Popular Preaching and Religious Authority
in the Medieval Islamic Near East

PUBLICATIONS ON THE NEAR EAST

Poetry's Voice, Society's Song: Ottoman Lyric Poetry
Walter G. Andrews

The Remaking of Istanbul: Portrait of an Ottoman City in the Nineteenth Century
Zeynep Çelik

The Tragedy of Sohráb and Rostám from the Persian National Epic, the Shahname of Abol-Qasem Ferdowsi
Translated by Jerome W. Clinton

The Jews in Modern Egypt, 1914–1952
Gudrun Krämer

Izmir and the Levantine World, 1550–1650
Daniel Goffman

Medieval Agriculture and Islamic Science: The Almanac of a Yemeni Sultan
Daniel Martin Varisco

Rethinking Modernity and National Identity in Turkey
Edited by Sibel Bozdoğan and Reşat Kasaba

Slavery and Abolition in the Ottoman Middle East
Ehud R. Toledano

Britons in the Ottoman Empire, 1642–1660
Daniel Goffman

Popular Preaching and Religious Authority in the Medieval Islamic Near East
Jonathan P. Berkey

Popular Preaching and Religious Authority in the Medieval Islamic Near East

JONATHAN P. BERKEY

University of Washington Press
SEATTLE AND LONDON

Printed in the United States of America

Library of Congress Cataloging-in-Publication Data

Berkey, Jonathan Porter.
Popular preaching and religious authority in the medieval Islamic Near East / Jonathan P. Berkey.
p. cm.—(Publications on the Near East)
Includes bibliographical references and index.
ISBN 0-295-98126-1 (alk. paper)
1. Islamic preaching. 2. Storytelling—Religious aspects—Islam. 3. Civilization, Islamic. I. Publications on the Near East, University of Washington.

BP184.25 .B47 2001
297.3'7'0902—dc21 2001027015

The paper used in this publication meets the minimum requirements of American National Standard for Information Sciences—Permanence of Paper for Printed Library Materials, ANSI Z39.48.1984

For Aidan and Olivia,
already, at ages six and three, master storytellers

Contents

Preface

Books come to be written for a variety of different reasons and in a variety of different ways. This book, like any other, had its own particular genesis, and it may help the reader to be aware of the circumstances that produced it. I hope that this narrative history of the project will also serve to recognize and acknowledge my debts to the individuals and institutions who helped see it to fruition.

After—in actual fact, even somewhat before—I had completed my monograph on *The Transmission of Knowledge in Medieval Cairo,* which was published in 1992, I came to be interested in the subject of popular culture, and especially popular religion, in the medieval Islamic Near East. That first book was a study of what some would call "high" culture, in this case, the organized and disciplined transmission of a body of texts and knowledge which formed the basis of both much intellectual life and the social and even political power of the religious elite in the later Middle Period of Islamic history. One of the most remarkable features of that system of transmitting religious knowledge, at least in medieval Cairo, was the degree to which those who were in some sense "outsiders"—that is, not by profession or occupation full-time religious scholars, or ulama—were nonetheless actively involved in the process of passing on the textual foundations of the faith and thereby maintaining the intellectual and ideological underpinnings of the medieval Islamic sociopolitical order. At the same time, through both my own reading of texts such as Ibn al-Ḥājj's highly entertaining *Madkhal al-sharʿ al-sharīf,* and also through the research of other scholars, most notably my friend and colleague Christopher Taylor's study of cemeteries and the cult of the "saints" in medieval Cairo, I became aware of just how extensively many of the ulama themselves actively participated in religious customs and practices that some (such as Ibn al-Ḥājj) thought of as illegitimate and dangerous, as decidedly "un-Islamic." It seemed to me that the two observations were intimately connected: that common people, for example, could share in the transmission of high culture was only the obverse of the coin, while the reverse demonstrated that the intellectual or academic elite could wallow in the "popular."

Consequently, when I began research on my next, and at that early stage rather unfocused, project, I hoped to invert the approach of my first book and to write the history of the transmission of religious knowledge in the medieval Islamic Near East, as it were, from the ground up. I was teaching at Mount Holyoke College at the time, and a grant from the college enabled me to spend a summer in London, combing through the manuscript holdings of the British Library. While there, I came across a number of interesting works, including an anonymous treatise (B.L. Or. 4275) entitled *al-Bāʿith ʿalā ʾl-khalāṣ min sūʾal-ẓann biʾl-khawāṣṣ* (The Enciter to Liberation from the Low Opinion of the Elite). A cursory survey of its contents indicated that the work was a defense of popular preachers and storytellers, a topic obviously of some relevance to a study of popular religion, so I had the manuscript copied and filed it away for future reference. In the meantime, however, another manuscript caught my attention. B.L. Or. 7528, which is missing both its first and last folios, and so is unidentified, is described in the catalogue as a "catechism on points of religion and morals, lives of the prophets, Muhammad, eminent Muslims, etc." In fact, what it seems to represent is the record of a popular preaching and storytelling circle.

I was fortunate enough, at that early stage of my career, to secure leave from my teaching duties on two occasions, first through a grant from the National Endowment for the Humanities (1992–93) and then through the generosity of the School of Historical Studies at the Institute for Advanced Study in Princeton, where I spent the 1994–95 academic year hallucinating that I had died and gone to historians' heaven. During those two years I continued my research into the broad area of popular culture and the Islamic religion in the Middle Period. Several studies emerged at that time, in particular an article laying out my initial thoughts about the relationship between different strands of medieval Islamic cultural activity which was originally delivered as a talk at various venues, including Indiana University, a seminar on "collective memory" at Princeton University, the University of Pennsylvania, and the 1995 meetings of the Medieval Academy of America; the article, which was eventually published in *Past and Present,* benefited from the comments of the various audiences. But the overall shape of a larger study was proving elusive. Finally, I began to focus on B.L. Or. 7528 and to organize and write a book-length study of the manuscript itself as representing a sort of "snapshot" of the kind of material and ideas which would have circulated in those gatherings in which nonelite Muslims received and transmitted religious knowledge. This book, as I envisioned it, would be organized around a series of related topics—"nature and cosmos," "words and the word," "poverty and secrets," "fear and hope."

That book has not yet been completed. After writing one chapter, I decided that an introductory study was necessary in order to set out the character and context of medieval Islamic popular preaching and storytelling circles, one of which produced the manuscript in question. That led me to go back and look more closely at B.L. Or. 4275. At first I did not know exactly what form this preliminary study would take—originally, I assumed it would emerge as an article—but, as J. R. R. Tolkien once said of his trilogy, *The Lord of the Rings,* "the tale grew in the telling." The result is this book.

A work that has had as long and tortuous a gestation as this one inevitably burdens its author with debts, intellectual and practical, which he can only dream of ever being able to repay. The initial research that has resulted in this book was made possible by the grant from the National Endowment for the Humanities. Most of my thinking on the subject and the organizing of the study was completed during my time at the Institute for Advanced Study in Princeton, an absolutely idyllic academic environment. I was especially fortunate that Michael Chamberlain and Maribel Fierro occupied offices just down the hall from mine; I drew shamelessly on the erudition and insight of both. The bulk of the book itself, however, was written in London during the summer of 1996, during a research trip made possible by a grant from my new employer, Davidson College. In the intervening years, portions of the book were presented in various venues. Chapter 3, in altered form, was delivered to a session at the 1997 meeting of the Middle East Studies Association sponsored by the Middle East Documentation Center of the University of Chicago and has subsequently appeared in volume 4 of *Mamluk Studies Review.* Chapter 4 was presented, at the kind invitation of David Wasserstein and Camilla Adang, at a workshop at Tel Aviv University in December 1998 on the topic of "Elites in the World of Classical and

Medieval Islam" and benefited enormously from the stimulating and challenging discussion that ensued. Meetings such as that at Tel Aviv are almost invariably the most productive settings for serious academic exchange, and I would like to thank its various participants, and especially Leah Kinberg, Daniella Talmon-Heller, Maribel Fierro, Ella Landau-Tasseron, and Julia Ashtiany Bray, for their extremely useful comments.

A variety of individuals have provided assistance in one form or another, some of them, perhaps, in ways of which they were not even aware, although none of them should be held responsible for any shortcomings in the final product. My failing memory will no doubt lead me to overlook some, but, in addition to those whose names I have already recorded, I would mention in particular Paul Cobb, Emil Homerin, Charles Issawi, Bernard Lewis, Shaun Marmon, John Meloy, Rachel Newcomb, Chris Taylor, and Michael Winter. I am especially grateful to the staff at the various libraries at which I have worked or from which I have obtained copies of manuscripts, especially the libraries of Princeton University and the Institute for Advanced Study in Princeton, the British Library, and the Bibliothèque Nationale. I am not the only member of the faculty at Davidson College to owe Joe Gutekanst, of the Interlibrary Loan Department at the college's E. H. Little Library, a profound debt of gratitude. Joe is the essential facilitator of much of the research in the humanities and social sciences which takes place in our small corner of the Carolina Piedmont. Michael Duckworth of the University of Washington Press has been patient and tolerant of my natural tendency (a professional hazard, one might say) to delay and to postpone, and the press's three anonymous readers saved me from a number of embarrassing errors.

Historians write books for their academic colleagues, but inevitably their families are drawn into their projects in one way or another. I am fortunate that my family has been so supportive of my work. My wife, Vivien, has shared with me the bewildering task of juggling our various responsibilities of research, teaching, and caring for young children. Both my parents and my in-laws have contributed their own time and effort—for example, by caring for our son in London during the summer of 1996 and so allowing me the invaluable opportunity to begin the writing of this book in close proximity to the sources on which it is based. Aidan and now Olivia have contributed to the project in their own way too, if only by constantly giving me good reason to smile.

Popular Preaching and Religious Authority
in the Medieval Islamic Near East

Introduction

One of the dominant themes of recent Western scholarship about the Islamic world has been that of the multiplicity and variety of religious experience and cultural expression within the Islamic tradition. In part, this has reflected a self-conscious effort to avoid the sin of essentialism, of assuming and asserting that "Islam" constitutes a clearly defined and substantially unchanging cultural entity, a sin of which an earlier generation of area specialists (identified pejoratively as "Orientalists") are often held to have been guilty.[1] Whether or not the academic Orientalists were, as a group, responsible for constructing such a monolithic understanding of Islam, and then bequeathing their flawed judgment to Western culture as a whole, as Edward Said and others have argued, there can be little doubt that the scholarly reaction to this *perception* of their mistake has been salutary.

The last several decades have witnessed a growing tide of academic studies exploring in depth aspects of the religion and culture of Muslims in various times and places, studies that do not rely upon essentialist assumptions but which seek to understand particular groups of Muslims, their lives and ideas, in specific social and historical settings. On one level, this represents simply the maturing of an academic discipline. On another, it reflects the way in which the discipline of anthropology, or at least ethnography, with its focus on the specific character of particular communities, cultures, and constructed systems of identity and meaning—what anthropologists have called the task of "thick description"—has profoundly influenced historical inquiry.[2] Anthropologists, said Clifford Geertz in his comparative study of Islam in Morocco and Indonesia, are "always inclined to turn toward the concrete, the particular, the microscopic. . . . We hope to find in the little what eludes us in the large, to stumble upon general truths while sorting through special cases."[3] Historians have increasingly followed in their footsteps.

One aspect of this process of maturation has been a movement away from narrative histories and studies of the "high" cultural tradition. Historians of Muslim peoples, both medieval and modern, have discovered "popular" culture. Some studies have focused on critiques of popular practices and rituals by generally hostile members of the ulama, the scholarly elite trained in the Muslim religious and legal sciences; others have made a broader effort to reconstruct popular culture from the ground up.[4] Beyond the distinction between high and popular culture, there lies the extraordinary and exemplary connectedness of medieval Islamic societies, at least those of the Near East. The practices and even personalities associated with one end of the cultural spectrum cannot usually be confined to it: scholars could be found participating in the very popular rituals associated with the cult of Muslim saints; common people participated, in some limited but meaningful way, in the transmission of religious knowledge; Sufi practices condemned by pious scholars have been shown to be intimately connected to, even derived from, mainstream Sufi values.[5] A variety of cultural practices, although experienced in different forms by different people in different venues, nonetheless shared certain commonalities that provided a kind of cultural "glue" sufficiently strong to bind together individuals and social groups of widely different circumstances and outlook. Any list of such shared cultural practices must include public moral exhortation. As with other areas of Islamic cultural activity, preaching transpired on a number of different levels, ranging from formal sermons during the Friday congregational prayers to street-corner harangues and the recitation of religiously edifying tales, and the differences between them are not always clear. Nonetheless, it is with the lower end of that range, a field populated with individuals identified in the sources as "preachers" (*wāʿiẓ*, pl. *wuʿʿāẓ*) or "storytellers" (*qāṣṣ*, pl. *quṣṣāṣ*), that this study is principally concerned.

The development of organized religious storytelling and popular preaching in the Islamic world was perhaps inevitable. In saying so, I do not by any means intend to repeat and affirm the racial prejudices and assumptions of nineteenth- and early-twentieth-century European scholarship about the "Semitic genius" for storytelling—the "keen eye for particulars," the "great subjectivity," the "nervous restlessness, deep passion and inwardness of feeling," which supposedly gave to the ancient Hebrews and the Muslim Arabs a "talent for lively and attractive prose narration."[6] Rather, I simply mean to draw attention to certain characteristic features of the religion of Islam and the sources available for the reconstruction of Muslim history. Islam, with the Sharīʿa at its heart, is an intensely ethical religion, and its moral imperatives drive Muslims both to self-improvement within the faith and to encouraging better "Islamic" behavior among their coreligionists. The Qurʾānic injunction to "command the good and forbid the evil" (*al-amr biʾl-maʿrūf waʾl-nahy ʿan al-munkar*) shoulders the believer with the obligation of implementing the religion's moral concerns and, by implication, with the task of discerning what exactly those concerns are.[7] Instruction on this point can be and is primarily sought from the Qurʾān, but the holy book can prove frustrating as a guide to correct belief and improved conduct. Its organization is, in some respects, arbitrary and confusing. With few exceptions, there is little narrative coherence in its recounting of tales of the prophets and other historical and pseudohistorical figures; the stories of Adam, Abraham, Jesus, and others are spread over many different *sūras.* Nor is there any convenient summary of its legal and ethical injunctions, nothing like a Decalogue or a Sermon on the Mount to capture and retain the attention of more casual readers or listeners. As a source of normative guidelines, the Qurʾān is to be supplemented by hadiths, stories about the words and deeds of the Prophet Muḥammad and his companions, but they too can prove bewildering. Not only do they cover an enormous range of issues and themes, but hadiths can be found to justify contradictory positions on a variety of questions.

Moreover, of course, these traditions naturally lend themselves to recitation and retelling of precisely the sort engaged in by storytellers and preachers. Not all of the prophetic hadiths boil down to simple and (perhaps) uninspiring injunctions such as "Any one of you attending the Friday [prayers] should take a bath" or "I have told you repeatedly to use a toothpick."[8] Entertaining stories about Abraham, Noah, Moses, and the other Israelite "prophets," as well as about Muḥammad and his companions, abound in most broad collections of hadiths. The precise historical relationship between such accounts and other literary genres common in the early Islamic record lies well beyond the scope of this study; it is enough for us to note that the telling of stories—in hadiths, in the accounts of the early Muslim campaigns (*maghāzī*), in tales of the Israelite prophets (*qiṣaṣ al-anbiyāʾ*), and later in the extensive biographical literature about scholars, pious Muslims, and other prominent individuals—has always played an important role in most channels of the Islamic literary tradition.[9] The role of stories was perhaps especially central to and identified with the tradition of exhortatory preaching: even a collection of "secular" tales such as the *Thousand and One Nights* contains a number of narratives of a devotional or exhortatory character.[10] In different contexts European historians have recently rediscovered the importance of stories to history. Lawrence Stone has spoken of a "revival of narrative" in historical writing, and Natalie Zemon Davis has investigated the strategic use of storytelling in archival sources themselves.[11] Historical writing about the Islamic world, by contrast, has always been heavily anecdotal, in part because of the importance of stories in the sources upon which historians must rely.

These two factors—the ethical imperative of the Islamic religion and the prominence of stories in the various literary genres—have contributed to making preaching a central part of the Muslim experience in most times and places. Such a statement can be made, I think, without lapsing back into "Orientalist" stereotypes and unsupported generalizations about the Islamic experience. Muslims always had before them, of course, the example of Muḥammad, whom the literary tradition frequently depicts exhorting and preaching to his people.[12] Next to the *miḥrāb,* the architectural niche usually assumed to indicate the direction of prayer, the *minbar,* or pulpit, is probably the most recognizable feature of a mosque, or at least of those mosques that, at noon on Fridays, provided the venue for communal prayers and delivery of a formal sermon, or *khuṭba;* unlike the *miḥrāb,* the *minbar* probably dates back to the period before the Prophet's death.[13] When an Iranian cleric climbs the pulpit in a mosque in Tehran to deliver a sermon on Friday, he does so in the conscious knowledge that he participates in a tradition that links him with earlier generations of religious leaders and with the Prophet himself.

The precise significance of the cleric's awareness, however, is somewhat problematic, and invoking it at this early stage of the present work raises a larger theoretical issue. In good postmodernist fashion, some have wondered whether the very notion of Islam may, as a practical matter, be overvalued, if not altogether useless. Is it possible to identify an "Islamic tradition" that provides any meaningful insight into seventh-century Arabia, ninth-century Baghdad, the glorious city of Cairo under the Mamluk sultans, as well as postrevolutionary Iran? Anthropologists have perhaps led the way in questioning whether a notion as broad as Islam or

Islamic civilization can provide any meaningful and significant insight into the diverse societies that label themselves Muslim.[14] Similarly, the preference among contemporary historians for tightly focused studies of Islamic societies has given rise to a suspicion of the very possibility of identifying an Islamic tradition or civilization as a meaningful framework for historical analysis. Edmund Burke III, for example, has provided an insightful critique of the unapologetically "civilizational" approach best represented by the late Marshall Hodgson. Burke acknowledged that Hodgson avoided the pitfall of ascribing "timeless" qualities to Islamic civilization and built into his model an understanding of Islamic history as a dynamic process through his emphasis upon the "dialogue" between different cultural strata. Nonetheless, Burke found the model unconvincing, in part because it is "too much the affair of Weberian virtuosos," atypical representatives of high cultural traditions rather than "ordinary Muslim men and women," and in part because Hodgson's concept of Islamic civilization rested too squarely on a set of moral values, the selection of which was, in the final analysis, purely arbitrary.[15]

Such objections can be met, I think, without abandoning entirely the heuristic value of the notion of an Islamic civilization. In the present case, for example, the study of popular preachers and storytellers inevitably moves away from the sphere of "Weberian virtuosos." Although some of the individuals who sermonized and related didactic religious stories to the common people were themselves prominent scholars of the sort who interested Hodgson, many of them, as we shall see, were not. Indeed, one of the most intriguing features of the practice is the enormous *range* of practitioners it attracted. Moreover, the subject of study was a practice, not a moral ideal; it represented a forum in which values were contested, perhaps, but which in itself made no assumptions about the ideal orientation of Islam.

But I think it important to assert more broadly at the outset that there *is* an Islamic tradition, a set of ideas, symbols, and interrelated texts and practices which may have a normative (although contested) force. It is true, of course, as anthropologists observe, that "religious symbols," including those that constitute the highly self-conscious Islamic tradition, "are normally expressed in a universal idiom whereas the experience of them occurs in particular times and places." Consequently, "the original historical circumstances [under which they were first enunciated] and the mentalities of later adherents inevitably differ, sometimes enormously, as also do their perceptions and their responses to the sacred message."[16] But this simply means that the true history of a religious tradition is to be sought in those moments of tension which arise as a result of its collision with the contingencies of historical circumstance and development. Even Geertz, for all his emphasis upon the particular and even countervailing historical forces at work in Morocco and Indonesia—the antipodes of the Islamic world, he called them—nonetheless acknowledged that both existed within an "ordered universe" and that the *meaning* of their historical experiences was to be gleaned at least in part from their relationship to that larger order. The task then of the anthropologist—or the historian—is to identify "the appropriate framework within which to view material phenomenally disparate in such a way that its very disparateness leads us into a deeper understanding of it."[17] Popular preaching and religious storytelling, I think, may constitute one such "appropriate framework," a point of entry allowing a detailed glimpse of the ordered but contested world of medieval Islam. Preaching and religious storytelling constitute a distinctive element of the Islamic tradition, and the practice cannot be understood outside that broader framework.

In our admirable rush to avoid hypostatizing Islam, we may miss the present reality that the construct has for those who identify themselves as Muslims. One anthropologist, while sympathetic in some ways with the arguments of his colleagues that, as a unit of investigation, Islam be replaced with a series of "local *Islams,*" warns that this approach "overlooks the underlying coherence manifest in the fact that Muslims, however seemingly diverse, all share elements of a common tradition. They characteristically assert their belonging to one *umma* [community] despite the fluid meanings they may attach to the categories related to it."[18] Those elements are various and diverse; they include, of course, literary texts such as the Qur'ān and the prophetic sayings, and practices such as prayer and preaching. The meaning and social significance of these elements are by no means clear and unproblematic: they will vary according to historical context and will frequently erupt with internal conflict. It is not for me, as a Western historian, to use such elements to define Islam; I simply observe that Muslims, in varying ways, commonly use them to define their own tradition.

My purpose here, I think, is not that far removed from that of Michael Gilsenan in his excellent study of modern Islam. Gilsenan insisted that his "aim is not to persuade the reader to substitute a relativized and fragmented vision for one of global unity. Rather it is to situate some of these religious, cultural, and ideological forms and practices that people regard as Islamic in the life and development of their societies."[19] Mutatis mutandis, that is my goal as well. Nonetheless, our approaches do differ somewhat. My topic, of course, is a medieval one, and the nature of the source material has its own imperatives—it may, for example, drive the historian to a slightly higher level of abstraction. But I am also, perhaps, slightly more interested in the explicitly Islamic character of these "religious, cultural, and ideological forms and practices that people regard as Islamic"—in what made them Islamic, and why Muslims contested their Islamic character.

The particular "practice" at issue here is preaching. This book makes no claim, however, to be a general study of preaching in the Islamic world. In fact, its pretensions are much more modest. It represents an effort to understand the tradition of popular preaching and storytelling, and the bitter controversy it engendered, in the central Islamic world (principally Egypt and the Fertile Crescent) during what Marshall Hodgson identified as the "Middle Period" (roughly 1000 C.E. to 1500 C.E.).[20] The scope of this study, its conceptual as well as geographical and chronological parameters, requires a few words of explanation. The issues can be conveniently grouped into four categories, the first of which is methodological.

In recent years scholars have vigorously debated the question of whether or not "popular culture" forms a distinct and coherent category of analysis. The question has received extensive treatment in the historiography of medieval and early modern Europe, in the work of scholars such as Peter Burke, Jacques LeGoff, Natalie Zemon Davis, and others.[21] Of late, several historians of the medieval Islamic Near East have also turned to a discussion of the issue. Boaz Shoshan, for example, has acknowledged the force of the argument made by the European medievalist Georges Duby and others that it is difficult if not impossible to draw precise lines between specific cultural phenomena and clearly delineated socioeconomic groups.[22] Indeed, such an argument probably applies with even greater force to the Islamic Near East, in which horizontal divisions between social groups (at least those that belonged to the dominant community of Muslims) arguably were more porous than in, say, the feudal societies of medieval Europe. On the other hand, Shoshan is of the opinion that such conceptual difficulties do not preclude the existence in the medieval Near East of a cultural stratum that can, in some meaningful sense, be said to reflect the popular. This stratum is embodied in "genres of 'texts,' both written and non-written . . . , which, despite their unavoidably uncertain boundaries, provide safe bases for analysis as primarily popular"—that is, which are the product of those "socially inferior to the bourgeoisie; hence, supposedly also illiterate, at least by and large."[23]

The question of literacy is of course a problematic one—in the medieval Near East, for example, literacy (at least for Muslims) almost certainly involved a diverse and sliding scale, rather than one dominated by a sharp distinction between those who could and could not read, since the importance of and ritual emphasis upon the Qurʾān placed a premium on a familiarity with the text and its language. But Shoshan's comments do remind us of the textual complexity of medieval Islamic culture. Much of what Western historians have written about the societies of the medieval Near East has rested upon the deceptively firm foundations of a particular textual tradition—that of chronicles, biographical dictionaries compiled by religious scholars, rarefied works of legal and religious scholarship, the literary legacy of accomplished poets and belletrists. But the story of medieval Islamic culture is more complicated and nuanced than this literary trail would suggest. It is cluttered with a bewildering variety of texts, including stories of saints' lives, accounts of the splendors of one city or region or another, personalized recountings of dream visions, rhapsodies on the qualities and even the supernatural powers of popular texts. Literary works such as these wreak havoc on the project of cultural archaeology, since they were acknowledged, sometimes even composed, by some representatives of high culture, and so confuse the stratigraphy of the literary remains. But many of them served to undermine, or at least to mute and to make contingent, the authority of that Islam that has been as much a construct of medieval ulama as of modern historians.[24] It is this, I take it, to which Shoshan refers in pointing to the popular as an analytically distinct, if not entirely discrete, stratum of Islamic culture.

Others have worried about the ideological assumptions behind the very category of "popular culture," particularly when dealing with matters specifically religious. Ahmet Karamustafa, for example, suggests that we should understand the antinomian and socially deviant behavior of groups such as the Qalandar dervishes as a new mode of piety, one that grew organically out of the values of mainstream Sufism in the Middle Period. To identify them instead as a manifestation of "popular religion," he points out, is implicitly to marginalize them and to suggest that they are somehow un-Islamic. Such an attitude is less the reflection of any real and categorical cultural distinctions than it is the product of one line of argument, associated with both medieval writers such as Ibn Taymiyya and Muslim modernists such as Fazlur Rahman, which has sought to identify one level of Sunni thought and practice as definitively Islamic.[25]

On the other hand, if we resist the ideological temptation of equating the popular with the timeless, with a cultural stratum that is "immune to historical change" and the domain of illiterate common people clinging "tenaciously to their ancient religious lore and ritual behavior,"[26] then what is loosely called popular religion would seem not to be altogether without promise as a field of historical analysis. On the contrary, if we assume that it is the very notion of an "orthodox" Islam, definitive for all times and places, which is problematic—whether that notion is the construct of defensive medieval theologians such as Ibn Taymiyya or an Orientalist tradition informed by the cultural assumptions of European history[27]—then it becomes possible to view popular culture and religion as a sphere of exceptional elasticity and fluidity, one that can be understood only in and through its specific manifestations.

So we can begin by agreeing with colleagues in European history that the study of religious culture must be "contextual and comparative," for only in this way can it be seen "in two-way communication with the structures of authority around it."[28] On the other hand, of course, the Islamic setting poses challenges, limitations, and opportunities of its own. For one thing, the sources available for historians of the medieval Near East are focused overwhelmingly on urban societies, and so the rural experience, which has been so rich a field for historians of popular religious culture in late medieval and early modern Europe, has remained more obscure. To date, at least, the historiography of the medieval Islamic world knows no parallel to the peasants of the village of Montaillou in Languedoc famously studied by Emmanuel Leroy Ladurie.[29] Even within an urban context, as we noted earlier, it is harder in the Islamic case to identify with precision particular social classes, at least as those classes have been understood in European societies, and so perhaps it is more difficult to study popular Islamic religious culture in the precise "relational" manner that European historians have urged.[30] Moreover, the practice we will identify in this study as popular preaching and storytelling seems to have cut across and been experienced by most, if not all, Muslim social groups. But in the apparent confusion lies the greatest opportunity for clarifying the specifically Islamic aspects of the problem. For example, the study of popular preaching may shed less light on relations between distinct social classes than it does on certain ambiguities in Islamic structures of religious authority and the dynamics of power relationships which those ambiguities engendered. And so what will emerge most clearly from this study, I hope, is a more nuanced understanding of the nature of that authority.

A second conceptual problem concerns the terminology employed by medieval commentators to describe the phenomenon of preaching. Ironically, the difficulty arises from the fact that preaching, or listening to preachers, was so enormously popular. We are not dealing here with a practice such as the continuing celebration in medieval Egypt of the pre-Islamic festival of Nawrūz or with self-consciously deviant behavior such as the Qalandars' ostentatious removal of all bodily hair. Rather, our concern is with a practice that was central to the religious experience of most, if not all, medieval Muslims.

Preaching took place on a number of different levels. On the grandest level there was the sermon (*khuṭba*) delivered during the Friday congregational prayers, in a mosque designed for that purpose (*jāmiʿ*), by a preacher *(khaṭīb)* often, although not always, representing or appointed by the ruler. These sermons, delivered from the pulpit (*minbar*), which constituted one of the few regular features of congregational mosques, followed fairly rigorous conventions regarding form and content—formulaic praise of God, prayers for Muḥammad and his community, recitation of Qurʾānic passages, and short admonitions to pious behavior.[31] Aḥmad b. ʿAlī al-Qalqashandī, author of a famous Mamluk period manual of administrative practice, commented that, of the various religious offices a scholar or jurist might hope to fill, that of saying the *khuṭba* was in fact "the grandest and highest in rank" (*ajall al-waẓāʾif wa-aʿlāhā*), because the Prophet himself had done it.[32] A saying of the Prophet urged care in stretching the attention span of listeners: "make your prayers [*ṣalāt*] long and your sermon [*khuṭba*] short."[33] In addition, of course, the Friday sermon had an explicitly political character. At least in the early decades of Islamic history, it was the usual practice for Muḥammad and, later, the caliph or his governor to deliver the *khuṭba* himself, and, although this practice had largely lapsed by the Middle Period, Muslims such as al-Qalqashandī retained its memory as an ideal.[34] Even after rulers generally abandoned the practice of delivering the *khuṭba,* the occasion retained its political importance, for the Friday sermon customarily included mention of the name of the ruler as a token of his legitimacy; failure to mention his name could amount to an act of rebellion.[35] The political function of the *khuṭba* as a public acknowledgment of a ruler's authority was one of the standard features of medieval Islamic polities of all stripes. On the first Friday after the conquest of Egypt by the armies of the Ismāʿīlī Fāṭimid caliph, led by their general, Jawhar, the preacher in the mosque of ʿAmr in al-Fusṭāṭ recited the *khuṭba* in the name of the Fāṭimid caliph al-Muʿizz, marking the arrival of the new dynasty.[36] Similarly, when the urban leaders of the eastern Iranian city of Nishapur turned the town over to the Saljūq Turks, the bulk of Nishapur's inhabitants learned of the event only several days later, when the *khaṭīb* said the Friday prayers in the name of the Saljūq sultan Toghrïl Beg.[37]

The *khuṭba* became one of the most characteristic and universal features of Islamic religious ritual. Preachers at the large congregational mosques in the major cities—such as the Umayyad mosque in Damascus, that of al-Manṣūr in Baghdad, or that of ʿAmr b. al-ʿĀṣ in al-Fusṭāṭ—were usually appointed by the ruler, and might attract thousands of worshipers to their audience on Fridays and major feast days. But a short address at noon on Friday did not preclude the possibility of preaching in other venues. Tāj al-Dīn al-Subkī, in his eighth/fourteenth-century survey of the responsibilities of the holders of various religious and secular offices, identified four different types of preachers: in addition to the *khaṭīb,* the *wāʿiẓ* (preacher, pl. *wuʿʿāẓ,* from a verb meaning "to admonish, warn"), the *qāṣṣ* (storyteller, pl. *quṣṣāṣ*), and the *qāriʾ al-kursī* (literally, "one who reads from a chair"). All in all, the distinctions al-Subkī draws have a formulaic, even artificial, air about them. With the exception of the political aspects of the *khaṭīb*'s sermons, to which he alludes, and perhaps their formal and precisely delineated venue, there is little to distinguish the four. The *wāʿiẓ,* al-Subkī wrote, had the responsibility of inspiring pious fear in his listeners and telling them stories of the early heroes of the Islamic faith (*al-salaf al-ṣāliḥīn*). The *qāṣṣ* would sit or stand in the streets, reciting from memory passages from the Qurʾān, hadiths, and stories of the early Muslims and encouraging his audience to pray, fast, and fulfill their other cultic and legal obligations. He must be careful not to recite what an unsophisticated public (*al-ʿāmma,* "the common people") might not understand, such as hadiths about the "attributes," *ṣifāt,* of God (presumably because of the danger of anthropomorphism) or passages from difficult theological or legal works. On the other hand, a similar injunction applied to the *khaṭīb,* who should avoid discussions that would be difficult for an ordinary listener (*ghayr al-khāṣṣa*) to comprehend and limit himself to treating "clear" (*wāḍiḥ*) matters. The *qāriʾ al-kurs ī*'s responsibilities were similar: he was to recite traditions, simple Qur'ānic commentary, and the like to the common people, although his name derived from the fact that, unlike the *qāṣṣ*, he would sit in mosques, schools (*madrasas*), and Sufi convents (*khānqāhs*) and read directly from books.[38]

What exactly do these various designations mean? Was there always a meaningful hierarchy of offices and functions, with a distinct group of people operating in an organized fashion to exhort and transmit basic religious knowledge to the common people? Here we must tread carefully. It seems that the office of *khaṭīb* customarily represented a specific post and function: that of delivering the sermon at noon on Fridays to the assembled congregation of Muslims. Throughout the medieval period, and down to the present day, individuals have been hired to discharge this duty in the congregational mosques of Muslim cities. The delivery of the *khuṭba* represented a coherent if limited tradition of religious discourse, and prominent medieval preachers such as Ibn Nubāta al-Fāriqī (d. 374/984–85) published collections of sermons which served as models for those who came after them.[39] Beyond this, however, the situation becomes much harder to pin down. Ibn al-Jawzī, a prominent preacher and critic of the preaching tradition, observed that, while terms such as *qāṣṣ*, *wāʿiẓ*, and *mudhakkir* (one who reminds his audience "of the blessing God has bestowed on them") originally had distinct meanings, in his day those meanings tended to blur, and the distinctions between them broke down.[40] Ibn al-Jawzī suggested that the term *qāṣṣ* in particular had come to embrace all three, although in fact *qāṣṣ* and *wāʿiẓ* are both fairly common in the medieval sources and are generally used there (and so will be here) more or less interchangeably.

The social historian must use terms such as *qāṣṣ* and *wāʿiẓ*, in part because the sources do and in part because social history is inevitably concerned with the individuals who play certain social roles. Nonetheless, doing so is in a way misleading, because the *quṣṣāṣ* and *wuʿʿāẓ* did not necessarily form a discrete social or occupational category. We must be careful not to reify terms that, for the medieval Muslims who used them, had more flexible, functional, contingent, and overlapping meanings. Terms such as *qāṣṣ* and *wāʿiẓ* should not be thought of as identifying categorical types but, rather, activities or even different aspects of the same activity, storytelling and preaching having both grown out of a common cultural soil. In this case the activity was the task of transmitting basic religious knowledge to, instilling piety in, and encouraging pious behavior among the common people, by which I mean that large body of Muslims who by nature, temperament, or profession were not clearly members of the ulama, the class of religious scholars and those training to be such. The common people might, of course, form a part or even the greater part of the audience for Friday prayers and the accompanying sermon, but such occasions by no means exhausted either their need for religious instruction or their curiosity for religious knowledge.

A third area of confusion arises from a common phenomenon in the societies and cultures of the medieval Islamic world, namely, the blurring of the boundaries between what appear to be, at first glance, discrete activities. In the first place, of course, storytelling was a disparate phenomenon, and the Islamic societies of the Near East inherited and adopted a long-standing tradition of storytelling of a purely secular nature. This literature took a variety of different forms: it was recited and recorded in both prose and verse, and it has survived as both epic narratives and more variegated collections of anecdotes. Edward Lane, in his classic, if dated, ethnographical study of Egyptian society in the early nineteenth century, drew attention to the important social role played by reciters of popular tales such as the fictional account of the life of the Sultan al-Ẓāhir Baybars.[41] There is a certain degree of overlap between such genres of entertainment, on the one hand, and the recitation of tales for didactic purposes and as a form of exhortation, on the other. This was a problem that bedeviled certain areas of religious discourse, especially that of hadiths, from an early period. By the third Islamic century a tradition circulated which clearly responded to the need some felt to distinguish between edification and entertainment: "Woe to him who spreads false hadiths to entertain the people."[42] But the confusion was endemic and could lend an air of religious gravity and significance even to tales apparently designed specifically for amusement. For example, some redactions of the *Sīrat ʿAntar,* an epic narrative concerning a famous pre-Islamic poet and warrior, begin with an account of the prophet Ibrāhīm drawn from the *qiṣaṣ al-anbiyāʾ*.[43]

Second, and more important, any effort to separate popular preaching and religious storytelling from the organized transmission of religious knowledge places strains upon the conceptual categories with which we seek to understand medieval Islamic culture. The centrality of knowledge and learning in medieval Islamic societies and the social uses to which religious knowledge and its transmission were put have given rise to a more extensive secondary literature than any other topic of medieval Islamic history.[44] One of the salient arguments of a recent study of higher education in late medieval Cairo was that people from various walks of life, including many who would not normally be thought of as members of the academic elite (the ulama), participated in some limited but meaningful way in the organized transmission of religious knowledge and texts.[45] With popular preaching and storytelling we encounter, as it were, the flip side of that coin. The texts transmitted by preachers and storytellers overlapped with those studied in classes in *madrasas,* mosques, and elsewhere. What little we can know about the texts and topics addressed in popular preaching circles will be discussed more fully (chap. 2); for now it is enough to observe that they might include Prophetic traditions, texts such as Abū Ḥāmid al-Ghazālī's catholic religious treatise *Iḥyāʾ ʿulūm al-dīn,*[46] and, of course, stories of the pre-Islamic prophets, which formed an important element in the edifice of Qurʾānic commentary, which itself constituted one of the major foci of a religious education. Formal criteria, too, can prove illusive as a means of distinguishing preaching and storytelling from education: classes and storytelling circles were both described by the word *sitting* (*majlis*) or *circle* (*ḥalqa*), and, unless the sources describe precisely the character of a sitting, it can be difficult to distinguish one type from the other.

The fourth and final problem concerns the sources used to reconstruct the activities of popular preaching and storytelling circles. The societies of the medieval Islamic Near East are in many respects well documented, but not all social activities or cultural phenomena can be reconstituted with ease from the sources at our disposal. Popular preaching and storytelling are particularly problematic in this regard. For instance, references to individual storytellers in the sources, especially the biographical dictionaries that are usually so rich a source for medieval social history, are understandably thin and scattered. As a result, it has been necessary to look for data in a wide variety of source material—for example, chronicles and biographical literature from sixth/twelfth-century Baghdad as well as ninth/fifteenth-century Cairo—simply in order to collect a sufficiently large body of evidence. This poses a certain danger, of course—namely, that of seeming to remove historical data too far from the contexts that produced it. But several factors make the effort worth the risk. The first, a negative one, is the thinness of the data from any particular time and place. A second is the structural similarities that characterized the explicitly Sunni, and frequently Turkish, military regimes that dominated the central Islamic world in this period, as well as the personal connections and shared outlook that bound together the Sunni ulama of the region. A third, perhaps the most important, concerns the subject of popular preaching and storytelling directly. Popular preaching came under sustained and coordinated attack from prominent figures within the legal and religious establishment in precisely this late medieval time frame. The best known of these critiques is that of the Iraqi scholar Ibn al-Jawzī (d. 597/1200), in particular his treatise *Kitāb al-quṣṣāṣ wa'l-mudhakkirīn,* but it was not alone; it directly influenced critical appraisals by Ibn al-Ḥājj (d. 737/1336), Zayn al-Dīn al-ʿIrāqī (d. 806/1404), Jalāl al-Dīn al-Suyūṭ ī (d. 911/1505), all residents of Egypt, as well as ʿAlī b. Maymūn al-Idrīsī (d. 917/1511), a Moroccan Sufi living in Syria. In a sense this tradition of criticism frames the present study, since it provided the context for a vigorous defense of popular preaching and storytelling which emerged from Egyptian Sufi circles at the end of the eighth/fourteenth or beginning of the ninth/fifteenth century (this text is introduced at the end of chap. 1). More generally, the criticism of popular preachers and religious storytellers formed one element of a broader attack on innovation in religious ritual and practice, which itself constituted one part of an effort by Sunni Muslim scholars to define the Islamic tradition more precisely, a project that was characteristic of the later Middle Period.[47] (I shall return to the question of the specifically medieval context of my topic at the end of the book.)

Moving beyond biographical and historical sources, and the polemical literature directed against popular preaching and other suspect religious practices, are there other texts that allow us to contact the phenomenon more directly? Those medieval sermons that have survived and have been published were produced largely by reputable, well-educated, and well-connected scholars, such as Ibn al-Jawzī.[48] Many bear the marks of being at least semiofficial. For example, the sermons of Ibn Nubāta, which have been reprinted many times, are very short, in ornate rhyming prose, and have a pronounced political element. Ibn Nubāta was *khaṭīb* at the court of the Ḥamdānid ruler Sayf al-Dawla in Mayyāfāriqīn and Aleppo, on the Byzantine frontier, and was known especially as a preacher of *jihād,* exhorting his listeners to holy war against the infidels across the border.[49] Preachers such as Ibn al-Jawzī were well known and held in high esteem, but the extent to which their sermons had an impact on those delivered by less famous and less well-trained practitioners is impossible to judge.

Nonetheless, sufficient sources do survive to permit at least a tentative study of the phenomenon of popular storytelling and preaching. There are, of course, collections of the tales that were popular in storytelling circles, the *qiṣaṣ al-anbiyāʾ,* collections compiled by individuals such as al-Thaʿlabī, al-Kisāʾī, Ibn Kathīr, and others.[50] Works such as these form a sort of literary pool from which preachers might draw, but in themselves are several degrees removed from spontaneous interaction with an audience. We may approach storytelling and preaching circles more directly in a collection of hadiths frequently transmitted by the *quṣṣāṣ,* compiled by Ibn Taymiyya, one of the leading Muslim polemicists of the Middle Period, and recently published under the title *Aḥādīth al-quṣṣāṣ.*[51] There is no reason to believe that his list is comprehensive, but it does represent a sort of "snapshot" of the material that an individual might encounter in a storytelling or preaching circle and so may help us to define the parameters of the religious knowledge generally available to nonelite, nonscholarly Muslims.

Direct records of the sort of preaching and storytelling circles that form the subject of this study are, of course, relatively rare, as the occasions were almost by definition fleeting. Nonetheless, some do survive and can help to fill in the skeletal picture derived from Ibn Taymiyya's *Aḥādīth al-quṣṣāṣ* and the polemical tradition. Among the more interesting is one associated with the preacher ʿAbd Allāh b. Saʿd Allāh, known as Shaykh Shuʿayb (or ʿUbayd) al-Ḥurayfīsh (or al-Harfūsh) (d. 801/1398–99), an Egyptian Sufi preacher connected to the shadowy underground brotherhood of the Ḥarāfīsh, who spent a number of years living and preaching in Mecca.[52] The people had "great faith" (*iʿtiqād zāʾid*) in him, according to the historian and jurist Ibn Ḥajar al-ʿAsqalānī, and he left to posterity a popular collection of short sermons and pious tales which has been reprinted several times in the modern period, a collection that goes by the title of *al-Rawḍ al-fāʾiq fīʾl-mawāʿiẓ waʾl-raqāʾiq* (The Splendid Garden of Sermons and Edifying Tales).[53] A more problematic document is an anonymous and incomplete manuscript housed in the British Library (Or. 7528). The manuscript is a random collection of tales, homilies, and brief excursuses on a variety of religious and legal topics. Since the manuscript is missing its first and last folios, it is impossible to say where it was from or when it was composed or even whether it was intended to constitute a single, integral literary work but what it seems to represent is a summary catalogue of what one individual heard—or transmitted—at a popular preaching or storytelling circle at some point in the later Middle Period.[54] One must be careful, of course, about drawing generalizations from a document of such uncertain provenance; on the other hand, B.L. Or. 7528 provides a level of detail and a sense of spontaneous contact missing from more formal, literary sources, whether those sources were hostile, like Ibn Taymiyya's, or sympathetic, like al-Ḥurayfīsh's.

With these methodological, terminological, and source problems in mind, we face a question: is it possible to analyze popular preaching and the transmission of religiously edifying tales as a distinct, if not discrete, aspect of medieval Islamic culture? Johannes Pedersen, an early Western student of Islamic preaching, argued that by the later Middle Period the storytellers had lost importance and that their functions had been absorbed by the *khaṭībs* and the Sufis. As proof, he cited the fact that al-Qalqashandī, in his enormous compendium of information for government scribes, did "not mention the *qāṣṣ* or the *wāʿiz* among the divine offices in Cairo, Damascus and Ḥaleb [Aleppo]."[55] But al-Qalqashandī's omission reflects only the fact that such individuals did not occupy, or only rarely occupied, formal posts in religious and educational institutions. Storytelling and exhortation in fact remained central to the spiritual life of Muslims in the Middle Period, even if the individuals who practiced it, and the forums and even the forms in which they did so, cannot always be identified with precision and clarity. The authors who compiled the enormous biographical dictionaries that are perhaps the most important source for social historians of the medieval Near East in general concerned themselves with individuals (scholars, jurists, sultans, and soldiers) of a more exalted rank than those who routinely preached and told stories to the common people. Nonetheless, these biographical dictionaries are littered with stray references to *quṣṣāṣ* and *wuʿʿāẓ* who caught their attention for one reason or another. As a rule, these references are unfortunately (but not surprisingly) brief, but they are common enough to indicate that the tradition of popular preaching and storytelling persisted.

Looking ahead, we might say that the tradition of popular preaching in the Islamic Middle Period was defined by three characteristics. In the first place, stories—in particular those of the pre-Islamic prophets, the *qiṣaṣ al-anbiyāʾ*, and of the pious early Muslims—formed the stock-in-trade of many popular preachers. Such stories were by no means restricted to the popular preachers, nor did they exhaust the latter's repertoire, but they did prove immensely popular with the audiences the preachers addressed, and so provided a helpful vehicle for the transmission of Islamic values and religious knowledge supportive of them. Second, and more important, the relationship of the tradition of popular preaching and storytelling to the more refined and disciplined transmission of religious knowledge was tentative and problematic but nonetheless real and unavoidable. The tension between them manifested itself on a variety of levels: that of topic (i.e., the nature and subject of the material addressed); that of authority (i.e., the means and criteria by which the legitimacy of the information transmitted was established); and that of personnel (i.e., the identity and training of those engaged in the transmission of religious knowledge). On all three levels the tradition of popular preaching and storytelling found itself in conflict with the disciplined transmission of religious knowledge and texts (what we might label, in the most tentative terms, "higher education");[56] at the same time, however, the two sociocultural processes could never be completely and hermetically isolated from each other. Third, the tradition of popular preaching and storytelling became, over the medieval period, increasingly intertwined with Sufism—on that point, at least, Pedersen was correct.

The surest proof of the persistence of a distinct tradition of popular preaching and storytelling is that it generated a considerable degree of criticism, which, as we have seen, formed a discernible theme of medieval religious polemic and which, along with the response to it, will form a principal focus of this study. That criticism, and the broader medieval polemic over blameworthy innovations and corrupt religious practices, implied a hierarchical relationship between that which was in some sense legitimately Islamic and that which fell short of recognized Islamic ideals. Since that polemic was produced by the scholarly elite, religious practices popular with the common people almost inevitably fell on the short end of the stick.

This points to a final observation that the reader should bear in mind. Islam, like any great religion or civilization, is too complex to be perfectly consistent; rather, it is fraught with competing and sometimes contradictory impulses and values. It is those very contradictions that generate the tensions that give the Islamic tradition vitality. On the one hand, it is frequently observed that Islam, which quite self-consciously possesses no sacerdotal class, realizes the Protestant ideal of a "priesthood of all believers" more perfectly than most Protestant sects. All Muslims, the Qurʾān makes clear in a famous passage, in the end stand before God as equals, distinguished only by the depth of their devotion to their Lord: "O you who believe, do not let one group mock another who may be better than they, nor one group of women another, who may be better than they. . . . O mankind, we have created you male and female, and made you into peoples and tribes, so that you may know one another. Truly, the noblest among you in the sight of God is the most pious. And God is All-knowing, All-aware."[57] Even the distinction between male and female is, in a sense, incidental: "Men and women who have surrendered [to God], believing men and believing women, obedient men and obedient women, truthful men and truthful women, patient men and patient women, humble men and humble women, men who are charitable and women who are charitable, men who fast and women who fast, men who are chaste and women who are chaste, men who remember God often and women who do so—for them God has prepared forgiveness and a great reward."[58]

On the other hand, medieval Islamic societies were arranged around a series of hierarchies. In legal terms, for example, those societies drew sharp distinctions between those who were, say, Muslim or non-Muslim, free or enslaved, male or female. In the religious sphere, hierarchies tended to form around the question of knowledge. The replication of religious knowledge, for example, through study, teaching, and the transmission of recognized texts, depended upon a system that, for all its flexibility and tendency to draw in and include as participants Muslims from quite different walks of life, spelled out clearly the grounds on which one transmitter of religious knowledge was to be preferred to another. Not surprisingly, therefore, the polemic over preachers and storytellers was ultimately a question of knowledge. The *quṣṣāṣ* and *wuʿʿāẓ* served the role of transmitting basic religious knowledge and instruction to the common people; the controversy that their activities engendered was in the final analysis about how the common people were to understand Islam.

1 / Origins and Early Controversy

As with many other Islamic institutions, the origins of the qāṣṣ *and the* wā'iẓ are obscure.[1] Later Muslim writers who discussed them related a number of differing accounts. Among the more common was one that identified Tamīm al-Dārī, a Christian convert to Islam, as the first person appointed to act as a *qāṣṣ*. According to one account, Tamīm twice asked the caliph 'Umar b. al-Khaṭṭāb for permission to act as *qāṣṣ* and twice was refused. On his third application the caliph granted his reluctant permission.[2] Tamīm, however, is himself an enigmatic figure, and the reports of his activities are encrusted with legend.[3] Other sources point to the caliphate of 'Alī, and the *fitna,* the period of social and political upheaval following the murder of the caliph 'Uthmān, as the time at which the storytellers first appeared; some lay the blame specifically at the feet of the Khārijī rebels, the militants who precipitated the first schism in Islam by breaking with 'Alī over his willingness to accept arbitration of his dispute with those demanding vengeance for 'Uthmān's murder.[4] The most recent study has concluded that these early reports yield little reliable information regarding the origins of organized storytelling but that the practice was certainly linked in a general way to the need to preach to and to teach the rapidly growing number of converts in the first decades of the Islamic state.[5] Muḥammad himself, of course, had instructed and exhorted his community, so it is hardly surprising that later Muslims followed his example.

In the first Islamic century the *quṣṣāṣ* operated at the center of the process by which the nascent religion defined itself, as the lines of political and legal institutions and authority only gradually came into focus. At the beginning they functioned as part of the network of individuals among whom Islamic law slowly took shape, answering questions concerning ritual and right behavior posed to them by members of their audiences.[6] The Umayyad caliphs quite naturally sought to control their activities. The office of the *qāṣṣ*, like that of the official Friday preacher, acquired a political dimension, and under the caliph Muʿāwiya became an official institution of the state, what Gordon Newby has called "the first salaried positions in Islam."[7] Stories related on the authority of Mālik b. Anas and others to the effect that ʿUmar b. ʿAbd al-ʿAzīz, generally regarded by the Sunni tradition as the most pious and reputable of the Umayyad caliphs, appointed storytellers and apportioned them monthly salaries suggest an attempt to give institutional form to the exhortatory impulse.[8] This did not, however, prevent unofficial and popular preachers from carrying on the task of spreading tales of the prophets and exhorting Muslims to what they considered correct behavior, completely independent of state control. In this growing tension lay the roots of later efforts to control popular preachers and storytellers and also of one of the most important textual weapons employed by the critics, a hadith in which the Prophet is reputed to have said that "only three kinds of people narrate stories: one who can appoint [*amīr*], one who is appointed for that purpose [*maʾmūr*], or a hypocrite [*murāʾī*]."[9]

Later criticism of the storytellers and popular preachers should not obscure the important role they played in the articulation and diffusion of Islam in the first Islamic centuries. A city such as Baṣra, for example, provided an open forum for their activities, and their audiences included both scholars (*fuqahāʾ*) and literati such as al-Jāḥiẓ.[10] In such venues storytellers and popular preachers became the principal channel of instruction for the common people, for those not engaged in a rigorous course of study of the religious sciences under the supervision of one or more scholars. Hence, those reports that indicate that it was the *quṣṣāṣ* who first began preaching "sermon-like accounts of an edifying nature" about the Prophet.[11] By the sixth/twelfth century, the Ḥanbalī jurist and theologian Ibn al-Jawzī, whose famous treatise on the storytellers, *Kitāb al-quṣṣāṣ waʾl-mudhakkirīn* (The Book of Storytellers and Those Who Remind [People of God's Blessings]), sought to rein in their excesses and set proper bounds for the material that they related, acknowledged their important role in the transmission of religious knowledge to the common people (*al-ʿawāmm*). Drawing on the ethical injunction related in the Qurʾān in *sūra* 3, verse 104, and elsewhere, he remarked that God had sent prophets "to draw people to the good and warn them against evil" and, after them, the ulama who are distinguished by their learning *(ʿilm)*. "Moreover," he said, "the storytellers and the preachers were also given a place in this order [*amr*] so as to exhort [*khiṭāb*] the common people. As a result, the common people benefit from them in a way that they do not from a great scholar."[12] At another point he was more precise: "The preacher brings to God a great number of people, while a jurist [*faqīh*] or a traditionist [*muḥaddith*] or a Qurʾān reader [*qāriʾ*] cannot bring [to God] a hundredth of that number, because [the preacher's] exhortations are addressed to both the common people and the elite [*liʾl-ʿāmm waʾl-khāṣṣ*], but especially the common people, who only rarely meet a jurist, so they discuss things with [the preacher]. The preacher is like the trainer of animals, who educates them, reforms them and refines them."[13]

Ibn al-Jawzī's simile was surely not intended to flatter the audience of common people who listened to the sermons and tales of the *quṣṣāṣ*. Nonetheless, it is clear from the polemics over preachers and storytellers that these "shepherds" often acquired a devoted following among their "flocks." According to a story told by Ibn al-Jawzī, the mother of Abū Ḥanīfa, jurist and eponym of the Ḥanafi school of law, refused to accept her son's ruling on a matter until his opinion had been confirmed by a storyteller in whom she placed great trust.[14] Ibn al-Jawzī related another tale concerning ʿĀmir al-Shaʿbī (d. c. 104/722–23), an Iraqi scholar who once entered a mosque in the Syrian city of Palmyra and there encountered "an elderly man with a long beard, around whom the people in the mosque had gathered taking down into writing what he said." When the old man repeated a hadith according to which "God has created two trumpets each having two blasts: the blast of death and the blast of resurrection," the visiting scholar could not help but correct him. "O Shaykh!" he said, "fear God and do not relate traditions which contain falsehood. God has created only one trumpet having two blasts: the blast of death and the blast of resurrection." The old man did not take kindly to al-Shaʿbī's intervention and struck him with his shoe. More important, his audience followed his example, and, according to al-Shaʿbī, "they did not stop until I had sworn to them that God had created thirty trumpets each having but a single blast."[15]

The devotion and loyalty of the common people to their preachers and storytellers is a theme that is repeated in discussions about them by Muslim scholars. It pervades, for instance, the treatise of the ninth/fifteenth-century polymath Jalāl al-Dīn al-Suyūṭī condemning the excesses of the storytellers,

Taḥdhīr al-khawāṣṣ min akādhīb al-quṣṣāṣ (A Warning to the Elites Concerning the Lies of the Storytellers).[16] In explaining the occasion for writing his treatise, al-Suyūṭī relates that he was asked about a storyteller who repeated hadiths that were not genuine. The hadith in question concerned *sūra* 21, verse 107, of the Qur'ān: "We have sent you [Muḥammad] as a mercy to the world." Muḥammad, according to the story, asked the archangel Gabriel whether any of that mercy had devolved upon him. "Yes," Gabriel responded, "before He created me, God created thousands of angels named Gabriel. He asked each of them, 'Who am I?' but they did not know what to reply, and so they wasted away. But when He created me and asked me, 'Who am I?' your Light, O Muḥammad, said to me: 'Say, You are God, other than whom there is no god.'" Al-Suyūṭī was of the opinion that this hadith was spurious and made his judgment known to the *qāṣṣ,* issuing a *fatwā* (personal legal ruling) to the effect that he must correct the traditions he recited under the supervision of reputable scholars. The storyteller reacted with rage, insisting that he desired the approbation of the people (*al-nās*), rather than that of the scholars (*al-mashāyikh*), and spurred on his listeners—al-Suyūṭī described them as the "rabble" (*al-ghawghā'*)—until they threatened to stone al-Suyūṭī.[17]

Such storytellers, according to al-Suyūṭī, defended themselves by accusing their scholarly critics of envy, a telling mark of the depth of the storytellers' popularity.[18] If the biographical literature is frequently reticent on the subject of preachers and storytellers, those whom the biographers did notice often stood out for the number of listeners drawn to their preaching. The historian al-Khaṭīb al-Baghdādī, who surely knew a good sermon when he heard one (his name means "the Baghdadi preacher"), described Abū ʿAbd Allāh al-Shīrāzī al-Wāʿiẓ (d. 439/1047–48) as one who "spoke to the people [of Baghdad] in the language of exhortation" and remarked that uncounted numbers attended his sessions.[19] Later in the fifth/eleventh century Abū'l-Ḥusayn Ardashīr al-ʿAbbādī al-Wāʿiẓ, passing through the Iraqi city after performing the pilgrimage, began to preach in the great Niẓāmiyya *madrasa.* His audiences, which included the famous scholar Abū Ḥāmid al-Ghazālī, increased in size until, Ibn al-Jawzī reckoned, their number reached thirty thousand.[20] Shihāb al-Dīn al-Sanbāṭī, who preached in the al-Azhar mosque in Cairo, did not perhaps attract crowds of comparable size, but his audiences were enthusiastic nonetheless. When he descended from his chair after his sermon, the people would jostle and fight with one another to draw close and touch him; if one of them was unable to touch the man himself, he would toss his girdle (*shadda*) so that it brushed against the preacher's robe and then draw the cloth over his face.[21]

Such individuals were clearly exceptional by any standards, but their success and popularity were replicated in varying degrees all the way down the scale of religious accomplishment and fame. The biographer of the famous Egyptian Sufi and preacher Ibn ʿAṭāʾ Allāh (d. 709/1309) remarked that "he was among those who talked [about religious subjects] to the people" and that individuals of all types, both "legal scholars" (*mutafaqqiha*) and the "common people" (*al-ʿāmma*), flocked to hear him speak.[22] Biographical notices of less famous preachers tend to be extremely terse, even in generally expansive collections such as *al-Ḍawʾ al-lāmiʿ li-ahl al-qarn al-tāsiʿ* (The Gleaming Light of the People of the Ninth Century) of the ninth/fifteenth-century Egyptian al-Sakhāwī, but it is not uncommon to encounter individuals who "sat with the people" and "preached to them" or "read to them." These transmitters of religious lore and exhortation often attracted the biographers' attention through the "confidence" (*iʿtiqād*) that their listeners and followers had in them. Ibrāhīm b. Miʿḍād al-Jaʿbarī (d. 687/1288), for instance, whose preaching was by all accounts eloquent, sat with the common people, and they had "confidence" in him. (Ibn Miʿḍād's popularity no doubt rested in part on what seems to have been a delightful sense of humor. When he was near death, he was carried out to the location of his tomb, in the Ḥusayniyya district outside Cairo, and said in a playful rhyme, "O little tomb, a little pair of buttocks has come to you.")[23] So did the preacher Ibn Bint Maylaq (d. 797/1395), a member of the Shādhilī order of Sufis, whose listeners also revered him—at least until he was appointed Mālikī *qadi* in Cairo, in which post he was found to have embezzled a fair sum of money.[24] Abū ʿAlī Ḥasan al-Khabbāz (d. 791/1389), another Shādhilī Sufi who, as his name suggests, began life as a baker, took up residence in a small mosque (*zāwiya*) outside of Cairo where he preached to the common people, on whose hearts his exhortations "left a mark" (*li-waʿẓihi taʾthīr fiʾl-qulūb*).[25]

Despite, or perhaps because of, their popularity with the common people, preachers and storytellers became the object of the wrath of more reputable scholars, as al-Shaʿbī's and al-Suyūṭī's experiences suggest. In fact, criticism of the storytellers forms a distinct focus of early and medieval Islamic polemical discourse.[26] In later chapters of this book I will discuss the issues raised by this polemic, as well as efforts to defend the preachers and storytellers, in greater detail. For the moment I wish simply to identify the general contours of the debate.

Criticism of preachers and storytellers was vigorous and sustained. One of their most persistent critics was the Ḥanbalī jurist and theologian Ibn al-Jawzī. Ibn al-Jawzī's attack on the lies preached by storytellers to their credulous listeners pulled no punches, and the author himself apparently judged his work a success by the malice that it stirred up among the *quṣṣāṣ*.[27] Ibn al-Jawzī was himself a preacher held in considerable repute by the people of his day and the author of numerous collections of sermons and treatises on the art of exhortation. With his large following among the populace of Baghdad who prized both his traditionalism and the eloquence of his sermons, Ibn al-Jawzī's career as a preacher was intimately connected to the fortunes of the ʿAbbāsid caliphs in their efforts to reclaim the power and authority that, under the Būyid amirs and Saljūq sultans, had slipped from their hands.[28] No doubt Ibn al-Jawzī's own experiences served as a graphic illustration of the power of preaching and of the preacher's capacity to affect not only the hearts of his listeners but the social and political structures of the day, giving an added urgency to the need to ensure that preachers got it right.

As his example should indicate, what earned the disapprobation of Ibn al-Jawzī and others was not preaching per se, nor reciting to gullible crowds stories about the Hebrew prophets or other topics of sacred history, projects that are an integral feature of Islam as experienced in most times and places; rather, it was certain practices, and excesses, of those who engaged in these activities. The attack came from various different quarters. Sometimes the critics objected simply to false preachers, to comic imposters who through their buffoonery drove their audiences to laughter, and in doing so, themselves skirted perilously close to unforgivable impiety: "they have all committed blasphemy," said the Mamluk period preacher Ibn Baydakīn al-Turkumānī.[29] Interestingly, in light of the later history of storytelling and popular preaching, many of the earliest critics were mystics. They included Abū Ṭālib al-Makkī (d. 386/996), who objected to the meetings of the storytellers on the grounds that they were inherently inferior to the *majālis al-dhikr* of the mystics, the latter being limited to those seeking mystical enlightenment through the disciplined mystic path, whereas the *majālis* of the *quṣṣāṣ* were open to anyone.[30] Later, when preaching and storytelling became closely associated with the Sufis themselves, critics complained of the wild emotionalism in evidence among the audiences at popular sessions, or the undue and indecent emphasis placed on love by these Sufi preachers.

But traditionists and jurists were also sharply critical of certain features of the storytellers' craft, and it was their objections that formed the central themes of the polemic against storytellers and preachers.[31] Many of those who denounced the storytellers or their excesses were themselves prominent transmitters of Prophetic traditions or adherents of a stridently traditionalist religious viewpoint, such as Ibn al-Jawzī, the Mālikī jurist Ibn al-Ḥājj (d. 737/1336), and the irrepressible Ḥanbalī scholar Ibn Taymiyya (d. 727/1328). Since much of what the preachers and storytellers recited took the form of hadiths, the concerns of their critics focused on the untrustworthy character of the material they transmitted. Ibn al-Jawzī worried that spurious hadiths (*mawḍūʿāt*) formed the stock-in-trade of many storytellers, and that the common people to whom they related them transmitted the unsound traditions to others, thereby compounding the damage.[32] In Ibn al-Ḥājj's opinion the fundamental error of the *quṣṣāṣ* was that they transmitted "weak sayings and stories" (*al-aqwāl wa'l-ḥikāyāt al-ḍaʿīfa*).[33] When transmitting accounts of the Muslim Prophet's words and deeds, of course, it was especially important to be careful and precise. Muḥammad himself was quoted as suggesting that no harm lay in telling unverifiable but edifying tales about the Banū Isrāʾīl, but that great evil would result from distorting his own words.[34] Ignorance was no excuse, but al-Suyūṭī was especially critical of storytellers and preachers who transmitted hadiths that they knew, or had reason to suspect, were false.[35] And the scope for error was enormous: some credited "heretics" (*zanādiqa*) with falsely attributing to the Prophet more than twelve thousand traditions.[36]

Dissimulation and dishonesty were characteristic of many storytellers and preachers, at least according to their critics. The traditionist Ibn Ḥanbal was quoted as saying that those most prone to lying and deceitfulness (*akdhab al-nās*) are beggars and storytellers.[37] The Andalusian Mālikī Abū Bakr al-Ṭurṭūshī, who settled in Alexandria, recounted a colorful anecdote about a hadith transmitter from Kufa, Sulaymān b. Mihrān al-Aʿmash (d. 148/765), who overheard a storyteller in a mosque in Baṣra recite a Prophetic tradition on his (al-Aʿmash's) authority. Al-Aʿmash entered the storyteller's circle and began to pluck out the hair in his armpit. The unidentified *qāṣṣ* challenged him, saying, "O shaykh, have you no shame?" The scholar cooly replied: "What I am doing is better than what you are doing, since what

I am doing is *sunna* [i.e., reflects the normative practice of the Prophet], while what you are doing is a lie and an innovation. I am al-Aʿmash, and I never recited to you what you have alleged."[38] Among the deceptions practiced by members of the Banū Sāsān, the shadowy brotherhood of the medieval underworld studied by C. E. Bosworth, was posing as a *qāṣṣ* or *wāʿiẓ* in order to win the confidence, and pick the pockets, of gullible audiences.[39] Zayn al-Dīn al-Jawbarī (fl. first half of the seventh/thirteenth century), in his colorful account of the Banū Sāsān, described their tricks: mounting pulpits, preaching on the terrors of the day of resurrection, and shedding tears "warmer than live embers," which they in fact produced by soaking crushed mustard seeds in vinegar, applying the concoction to their handkerchiefs, and then using them to wipe their faces, which of course caused their tears to flow "like rain"; or planting in their audience a man posing as a Jew or Christian who, in response to the sermon, rose to proclaim his conversion to Islam and his encounter with Muḥammad in a dream, the Prophet urging him to seek out the preacher and have him instruct him in the forms of prayer and the precepts of the true religion—all of which, of course, impressed the audience with the preacher's holiness and conned them into passing the hat on his behalf.[40] The Banū Sāsān were, of course, professional imposters, but the problem was that, in the protean world of popular culture, there was often little to distinguish them from other practitioners of the arts of storytelling and preaching. Ibn al-Jawzī accused the *quṣṣāṣ* of feigning an indifference to worldly goods as a devious method of persuading their audiences to pay them even more for their services, and al-Suyūṭī disparaged them as "swindlers" (*ghashshāsh).*[41] According to the critics, greed was not limited to street corner or soapbox orators: Ibn al-Jawzī condemned the Sufi Aḥmad al-Ghazālī (a famous preacher and brother of Abū Ḥāmid) for demanding as much as one thousand dinars in payment for reciting a sermon, while a tenth/sixteenth-century treatise reported that no appointment as Friday preacher (*khaṭīb*) could be had in Syria or Egypt without payment of a substantial bribe.[42]

Complaints about the honesty of particular preachers, however, or even of preachers and storytellers as a group, have a certain rhetorical air to them. Ibn al-Ḥājj, for example, in the early eighth/fourteenth century, complained about preachers who staged fraudulent confessions to impress their audiences in terms that parallel directly the earlier account of al-Jawbarī.[43] A more biting and formal criticism, and one that was repeated over the centuries, was that storytelling itself was in some way an "innovation" (*bidʿa*) and therefore suspect and dangerous. This concern is implicit already in the traditions about the origins of the practice, such as those that depict Tamīm al-Dārī as pestering the caliph ʿUmar to condone a novel practice. Sometimes the scholars' anxieties focused on particular practices associated with the *quṣṣāṣ,* such as their singing verses of the Qurʾān "beyond the proper bounds" (*al-qirāʾa bil-alḥān al-khārija ʿan al-ḥadd al-maʾlūf*) or their transmission of heretical innovations in the form of what they claimed were hadiths.[44] But others saw the practice generally as an illicit innovation. Thus, for example, al-Suyūṭī pointedly began his treatise against the "lies of the *quṣṣāṣ*" by citing a hadith in which the Prophet condemned innovations, while rigorous Mālikī critics such as Ibn al-Ḥājj saw the practice of storytelling itself as novel and a threat to the Islamic social order.[45]

Not all scholars, of course, saw all innovations as necessarily bad. Ultimately, most jurists came to distinguish between innovations that were "good" or "praiseworthy" and those that were "bad" or "blameworthy," while some developed a more refined hierarchy according to which innovations were ranked on a scale from forbidden (*muḥarrama*) to mandatory (*wājiba*).[46] Nonetheless, suspicion of that which was new and not grounded in Prophetic practice was a common element in medieval Islamic discourse, and one that over time grew stronger and more insistent. Efforts to employ the latent suspicion of innovations to discredit storytellers and preachers reflect the seriousness with which medieval writers approached the issue. The *qāṣṣ,* according to a hadith quoted by opponents of the storytellers, can anticipate only God's wrath on the Day of Judgment. There were doubts about the authority of the tradition, but the scholars repeated it anyway as a "warning" (*tarhīb*).[47] Ibn al-Jawzī linked the practice of storytelling to the destruction of the nation of the Banū Isrāʾīl, and warned those who undertook the practice that God would judge them severely if they led their listeners astray.[48] The reference to the evil fate of the Banū Isrāʾīl is a reminder that the critics viewed the issue as one that concerned not merely the fate of individuals but the social and political order itself—so, for example, the linkage, in hadith and in later polemics, of storytelling and preaching with *fitna,* social strife. And so the early tenth/sixteenth-century Sufi ʿAlī b. Maymūn al-Idrīsī could employ the language of *jihād* against the storytellers and others who corrupted the transmission of religious knowledge, asserting that "striving against them in holy war is more meritorious than doing so against the unbelievers of the House of War [i.e., unconquered territories outside the House of Islam], as the evil they inflict is greater than that of the people of the House of War."[49]

One of the reasons ʿAlī b. Maymūn held popular preachers and storytellers in such venomous contempt was his perception that their popularity with all ranks of Muslim society threatened the gender boundaries that cut across the medieval Islamic world. In his opinion the common practice of men and women gathering in a mosque to hear a preacher (*wāʿiẓ*), without any partition between them (*bi-ghayr ḥijāb*), posed a more insidious danger to Islam than adultery or wine selling, since any Muslim—elite or commoner, male or female, slave or free—would know that the latter two are forbidden. To make matters worse, those who indulged in this unregulated mixing of the sexes apparently did so with the full intention of exploiting the occasion: the women who attended often perfumed themselves and dressed in their finery, bedecking themselves with jewels to increase their attractiveness to men.[50] ʿAlī b. Maymūn's concerns were by no means idiosyncratic. Ibn al-Jawzī had condemned the mixing of men and women in preaching circles several centuries earlier.[51] And, of course, Ibn al-Ḥājj viewed the practice in the most colorful, apocalyptic terms. He shuddered at the thought of the "rending of the sacred [boundary separating men and women]" (*hatk al-ḥarīm*) among the mixed-gender audiences listening to preachers and speculated about the evil things that transpired "on moonlit nights" (*fiʾl-layālīʾl-muqmira*) in the great cemeteries outside the city of Cairo by preachers and storytellers plying their trade.[52] The liberties indulged in by the preachers' listeners threatened not only formal gender boundaries but all standards of decency and propriety. Sometimes they shouted aloud, said Ibn al-Jawzī, as if seized by an ecstatic experience (*wajd*): female members of the audience might "cry out like the crying of a pregnant woman at the time of her delivery. At times they even throw off their outer garment and stand up."[53]

Storytelling and preaching circles represented transgender spaces in another sense as well, since women might also lead them. Medieval compilers of biographical dictionaries occasionally mentioned individual women who served as preachers. The term most commonly employed was simply the feminine form of *preacher*—*wāʿiẓa*—and, while such biographical entries generally contain precious little contextualizing information, they may relate enough to indicate that these women were respected for their learning and piety: the woman might be described as "reliable" (*ṣādiqa*) or "virtuous" (*ṣāliḥa*), or she might be identified as a recognized transmitter of hadiths.[54] But others saw this as a dangerous intrusion upon male authority. Ibn al-Ḥājj, for example, condemned those "shaykhas" who acted as *quṣṣāṣ*. He noted that even men who read and understand books are rarely free from dissension and error—what then can be said of a woman who is "crooked, root and branch" (*muʿwajja aṣl^an wa farʿ^an*), who has read little (*qalīlat al-muṭālaʿa*), who is unable to distinguish the "sound" (*ṣaḥīḥ*) from the "unsound" (*saqīm*), and who may in fact have fallen into "pure unbelief" (*al-kufr al-ṣarīḥ*)? The danger is especially great since the "stories and tales" (*al-qiṣaṣ waʾl-ḥikāyāt*) they tell are unsound and fraught with lies. Ibn al-Ḥājj's despair was almost complete, as he commented sadly that he had heard of a case in which such outrages had occurred even in the home of "one of the esteemed scholars" (*shaykh min al-shuyūkh al-muʿtabarīn*).[55]

The polemical discourse over preachers and storytellers is dominated by their critics, but these transmitters of religious lore and knowledge to the common people were not without their defenders. One treatise written to justify them is *al-Bāʿith ʿala ʾl-khalāṣ min sūʾal-ẓann biʾl-khawāṣṣ* (The Enciter to Liberation from the Low Opinion of the Elites—i.e., the elite scholars who scorned popular preachers and storytellers), a work that exists in a single anonymous manuscript in the British Library (Or. 4275).[56] This treatise contains a point-by-point response to a critical tract penned by Zayn al-Dīn ʿAbd al-Raḥīm al-ʿIrāqī (d. 806/1404), a Shāfiʿī jurist and traditionist who lived most of his life in Egypt. Al-ʿIrāqī's polemic, entitled *al-Bāʿith ʿalāʾl-khalāṣ min ḥawādith al-quṣṣāṣ* (The Enciter to Liberation from the Innovations of the Storytellers), has apparently not survived, although al-Suyūṭī's *Taḥdhīr al-khawāṣṣ* as well as B.L. Or. 4275 contain extensive excerpts.[57]

Zayn al-Dīn al-ʿIrāqī cut a prominent figure among the ulama of late-eighth/fourteenth-century Cairo.[58] Born into a family of Kurdish origin, from a village near Irbil, his father brought him to Egypt in his youth and took special care with the education of his son. Zayn al-Dīn studied the variant Qurʾān readings, jurisprudence and its methodology, but above all hadith. His father was careful to ensure that his son received *ijāzas* (licenses) attesting that he had studied traditions with and received permission to transmit traditions from the leading authorities of the day. His academic record reads like that of a model late-medieval religious scholar. He traveled widely and frequently, for instance, to study with the ulama of Syria and the Hijaz, his efforts made more efficacious by the fact that he had a prodigious memory and was able to memorize up to four hundred lines of text per day. He held a number of teaching posts in the leading academic institutions of Cairo and served as both judge and Friday preacher in Medina. His colleagues accorded him considerable respect: one of them reported having a dream in which he saw the Prophet standing with Jesus on his right hand and al-ʿIrāqī on his left.[59]

That Zayn al-Dīn should fancy himself a defender of the integrity of the religious knowledge represented by hadith, the science of jurisprudence, and the like, and of its transmission, is perfectly understandable. But that in itself need not imply hostility toward popular preaching and storytelling. On the contrary, it appears that both Zayn al-Dīn and his son were intimates of various individuals of the Bulqīnī family, another prominent scholarly dynasty whose members had, as we shall see, a special concern with preaching and transmitting religious lore to the common people.[60] His objections, therefore, were presumably directed not at popular preaching and storytelling themselves, but at certain peculiar features characteristic of their practitioners in eighth/fourteenth-century Cairo and, in particular, at the influence on them of Sufi mysticism.

It comes as no surprise, then, to find that the anonymous treatise rebutting his own is itself infused with Sufi values. Moreover, it is possible now to identify its author as one of the leading mystics of late-eighth/fourteenth-century Cairo. There is little internal evidence of authorship in the text itself. The author observes that "storytelling" (*qaṣaṣ*) refers to "gathering the people together with one who instructs them in what is good, as," he says, "people would gather with my father during Ramaḍān."[61] His father, in other words, was a practitioner of the art. Virtually the only piece of evidence tying the work to a particular place is the certification on the final page of the manuscript that an individual named Muḥammad Fatḥ Allāh b. Maḥmūd al-Bīlūnī [?] al-Makanī [?] completed his reading of the text with an unidentifiable Abū'l-Ṣalāḥ, the "servant" (*khādim*) of the tombs of the Banū'l-Wafā'. That, however, is an important clue. The Banū'l-Wafā' refers to the family of Sufi *shaykhs* descended from Sīdī Muḥammad b. Wafā' (or Muḥammad Wafā') (d. 765/1363–64). Sīdī Muḥammad was an illiterate but eloquent mystic, the author (despite his lack of formal education) of "many compositions" (*muʾallafāt kathīra*) who, according to legend, received his cognomen of Ibn Wafāʾ after successfully ordering the Nile River, which had failed to rise, to complete (*awfā*) its annual innundation.[62] His descendants served as *shaykhs* of what came to be known as the Wafāʾiyya, a branch of the important Shādhiliyya order of mystics. The Wafāʾiyya developed a widespread reputation as preachers; Abūʾl-Fatḥ Muḥammad (d. 852/1448), grandson of the original Sīdī Muḥammad, for example, attracted to his circle prominent scholars and even the ruling sultan, as well as the common folk.[63] The Wafāʾī order attracted an especially large number of adepts from the Maghrib; nonetheless, the Wafāʾiyya survived into the twentieth century as one of the leading Sufi orders in Egypt, serving also as the corporation of those claiming descent from the Imām ʿAlī b. Abī Ṭālib.[64] The "tombs" of the Banūʾl-Wafāʾ were contained in a mosque at the foot of the Muqaṭṭam hills and held the remains of Muḥammad b. Wafāʾ, his son ʿAlī, and other members of the family. The mosque served as the principal *zāwiya* of the Wafāʾiyya, and was extensively restored by the Ottoman vizier Ezzet Mehmet Pasha at the order of Sultan Abdulhamid I in 1191/1777–78.[65]

So the treatise defending storytellers circulated among this important order of dervishes; in fact, the connection was much closer. The author of the treatise was almost certainly ʿAlī b. Muḥammad b. Wafāʾ (d. 807/1404), the famous son of the founder of the order. ʿAlī was one of the most popular and influential mystics and preachers in Egypt at the turn of the ninth/fifteenth century.[66] The prolific tenth/sixteenth-century Sufi ʿAbd al-Wahhāb al-Shaʿrānī gave him an unusually long entry in his biographical dictionary of famous mystics; the first thing he reports is that ʿAlī was extremely attractive, that Egypt had never known anyone as beautiful "in his face or his dress" (*wajh*^{an} *wa-lā thiyāb*^{an}). More important, we are told that ʿAlī studied both literature (*adab*) and the art of preaching (*waʿẓ*) and that his compositions included collections of poetry and sermons. Indeed, in addition to *al-Bāʿith ʿalā ʾl-khalāṣ*, he has left a number of treatises dealing with Sufi mysticism as well as a sizable *Dīwān* of his religious poetry, works all still in manuscript.[67] His younger contemporary, the historian and jurist Ibn Ḥajar al-ʿAsqalānī, noted that among his writings was a treatise to which he gave the title *al-Bāʿith ʿalā ʾl-khalāṣ fī aḥwāl al-khawāṣṣ* (The Enciter to Liberation from the Concerns of the Elites)—almost, but not quite, the title on the manuscript B.L. Or. 4275. Ibn Ḥajar's pupil, the biographer al-Sakhāwī, goes on to say, however, that

Zayn al-Dīn al-ʿIrāqī's treatise against the storytellers was directed specifically at ʿAlī b. Wafāʾ and that ʿAlī had composed his own work in direct response to his critic. That would seem to indicate that the anonymous treatise preserved in the British Library was in fact authored by the head of the Wafāʾiyya order in Egypt in the late eighth/fourteenth or very early ninth/fifteenth century. This identification should allow us, in the chapters that follow, to understand more fully the debate over the role and legitimacy of popular preachers and storytellers in late medieval Islamic society.

2 / Storytelling and Preaching in the Late Middle Period

ʿAlī Pashā Mubārak, in his exhaustive survey of the landscape and monuments of nineteenth-century Egypt, described the "mosque of the Wafāʾī masters." This institution, originally serving as a small retreat (*zāwiya*) for the Wafāʾīs, had been reconstituted and endowed as a more formal place of prayer (*masjid*) by the Ottoman vizier Ezzet Mehmet Pasha in 1191/1777–78, by order of the Sultan Abdelhamid. In the precincts of the mosque, which still exists, is a tomb (*maqṣūra*) containing the remains of ʿAlī b. Wafāʾ and his father; other members of the family were also buried within the complex. The mosque is located at the foot of the Muqaṭṭam hills, to the east of the tomb-shrine of the Imām al-Shāfiʿī—that is, within the extensive network of cemeteries that ring the city of Cairo to its south and east.[1] These cemeteries had been, since the Middle Ages, places of considerable activity of a social, economic, cultural, and religious character. The area contained, in addition to tombs, a number of important structures devoted to worship, education, or Sufi practice. It comes as no surprise, therefore, to find within it a mosque serving as a gathering place for a Sufi order and the scene of much devotional activity—worship and acts of Sufi ritual, the transmission of texts such as ʿAlī b. Wafāʾ's defense of storytellers, and, no doubt, preaching.

The Wafāʾī mosque was by no means the only center of preaching in the great Cairene cemeteries. Ibn al-Ḥājj was deeply critical of much that went on in the cemeteries—he worried, for instance, that the muleteers who transported women to the graveyards to visit the tombs of Muslim saints would slip their hands over their charges' thighs and shoulders and that men and women would meet there alone at night, in a place with plenty of cells (*khalawāt*) and empty spaces—and one of his concerns was that preaching circles in the cemeteries provided an opportunity for illicit behavior. Storytellers and preachers, he remarked, could often be found plying their trade in the cemeteries on moonlit nights.[2] Such gatherings were especially common on the various religious holidays and festivals, such as that of the Prophet's birthday (*mawlid*). On these occasions men and women would gather with preachers of either sex for riotous sessions marked by wailing, shouting, and crying, when the preachers, transported by the emotional force of their sermons, might be seized by physical convulsions on the pulpits or chairs on which they sat: their hearts, and those of their audience, said Ibn al-Ḥājj, were "bewitched" (*maftūna*), and they indulged in practices "unbecoming to believers." Indeed, it is his discussion of such behavior which provided Ibn al-Ḥājj with the occasion for his most extensive condemnation of the practice of storytelling itself, of those who claimed to be well versed in Qurʾānic exegesis and the stories of the prophets but who in fact corrupted the tales that they told.[3]

The historian must be careful not to mistake Ibn al-Ḥājj's vitriolic treatise as a definitive description and analysis of eighth/fourteenth-century Cairene social life. The Mālikī jurist had a personal agenda and concerns that deeply colored his view of the society in which he lived. His treatise reveals an obsessive fear, for example, of the unregulated mixing of men and women, a fear that is reflected in his treatment of preaching and storytelling in the cemeteries and on religious holidays, whether in his ungenerous estimation of female preachers or his vivid imagining of sexual transgression by members of the preachers' audiences.[4] But neither are his observations to be dismissed as without value. His criticism of preachers and storytellers active in the cemeteries and on religious holidays points to one end of a broad spectrum of channels by which religious lore and knowledge was transmitted to the common people of the city. The cemeteries were popular as a forum for such transmission because of the relative freedom that they represented: just as they lay beyond the walls of the city, so did they lie beyond the limits of effective regulation by religious or secular authorities, however that control might be exercised.[5] But the nature of that transmission did not differ significantly in character from that which transpired elsewhere: as we have seen, Ibn al-Ḥājj himself remarked that the activities he described and condemned occurred in the houses of respectable scholars as well as in cemeteries.[6]

Preaching and storytelling were activities that were undertaken in a variety of venues. Most obviously, of course, there were the preachers who were appointed in various mosques to deliver the Friday sermon required by Islamic law. By the later Middle Period the older ideal that each community should have only one congregational mosque for the saying of Friday prayers had long since broken down, and numerous mosques, both large and small, employed *khaṭībs* to deliver the Friday sermon. In Mamluk Cairo the *khuṭba* might be delivered by more than one hundred men on any given Friday, in mosques as well as religious schools (*madrasas*) and Sufi convents (*khānqāhs*). The Mamluk-period Egyptian scribe al-Qalqashandī, in his manual of administrative practice, admitted that he could not enumerate the number of mosques in which the Friday sermon was now delivered. This sort of preaching obviously did not require full-time employment, and many of those who received appointments as *khaṭīb* at one mosque or another worked in other religious or legal positions during the week.[7]

On a more general level scholars transmitted religious knowledge to and exhorted the common people in a setting that the sources refer to as *mīʿād*.[8] This term, which literally means only "appointment" or "appointed time," was a flexible one. On the one hand, it could indicate a specific post in a particular mosque, or *madrasa*. Quite a few religio-academic institutions in late medieval Cairo employed individuals to perform the *mīʿād*, to read from collections of traditions, books of Qurʾānic exegesis, accounts of the pious early Muslims, and exhortatory works to individuals from varying social backgrounds assembled for the session. But the term did not necessarily refer to a formal post; it could also indicate simply an activity, one that was essentially similar to preaching and storytelling. Jalāl al-Dīn al-Suyūṭī pointedly referred to the session presided over by the unscrupulous storyteller whose reckless transmission of hadith persuaded the scholar to compose his treatise *Taḥdhīr al-khawāṣṣ* as a *majlis mīʿād*.[9] The activity is frequently associated in the sources with individuals who are otherwise identified as "preachers," such as Shihāb al-Dīn Aḥmad b. ʿUmar, known as al-Shābb al-Tāʾib (The Penitent Youth) (d. 832/1428–29), who led *mīʿād* sessions in the al-Azhar mosque as well as in *zāwiyas* that he established in both Damascus and Cairo specifically for that purpose, sessions to which the common people flocked.[10] Quṭb al-Dīn ʿAbd al-Munʿim b. Yaḥyā al-Wāʿiẓ (d. 697/1297–98), Friday preacher at the al-Aqṣā mosque in Jerusalem, also held a regular *mīʿād* session after morning prayers in which he recited Qurʾānic exegeses from memory.[11] By contrast, Burhān al-Dīn Ibrāhīm al-Ḥulwānī (d. 791/1389), a preacher in Cairo "after whom no one performed the *mīʿād* [lit., *al-mawāʿīd*, the plural form] so beautifully," was singled out for having never preached "except from a book."[12] Confirming the essential identification of *mīʿād* with preaching, after Ṣāliḥ b. ʿUmar al-Bulqīnī (d. 868/1464) led a well-received *mīʿād* session, someone composed as a tribute the verses:

> Our imam preached [*waʿaẓa*] to mankind—the eloquent man who poured out the sciences like an ocean filled to overflowing and healed hearts with his knowledge and his preaching for only the preaching of a righteous man [*ṣāliḥ*] can heal.[13]

As the last several examples should suggest, the term *mīʿād,* like *preaching* and *storytelling* more generally, was not necessarily used by the medieval historians and biographers, who themselves were for the most part products of the learned elite and who shared their values, in contexts that imply criticism or disapproval. Indeed, the practice was undertaken by many individuals famed for their probity and scholarship, most notably a series of members of the Bulqīnī family of Cairo, who performed the *mīʿād* in a number of the city's *madrasas,* including one established by the Bulqīnīs themselves. The patriarch of this family was the father of the aforementioned Ṣāliḥ, Sirāj al-Dīn ʿUmar b. Raslān (d. 805/1403), a prominent traditionist and Ḥanafī jurist. Like other members of his family, Sirāj al-Dīn ʿUmar appears to have felt a special calling to spread knowledge widely among the populace; as a result, he had an excellent reputation among the common people, who flocked to him seeking *fatwās* in response to particular problems or questions that they faced.[14] His experience, as well as that of his sons and grandsons, confirms a close connection between *mīʿād* and Qurʾānic exegesis (*tafsīr*), for one of his biographers recorded that "in his *mīʿād* sessions, he completed his reading of the Qurʾān, infusing it with preaching [*waʿẓ*] which, God willing, was helpful [to his listeners]."[15] An older son, ʿAbd al-Raḥmān, replaced his father as head of a *mīʿād* circle in the Ḥijāziyya *madrasa,* beginning his exegesis with the last verse of the Qurʾān upon which ʿUmar had expounded; some years later ʿAbd al-Raḥmān himself died after reaching the very same verse in his own cycle of exposition.[16]

This last point, on the connection between *mīʿād* and *tafsīr,* is particularly instructive. In the first place it should remind us of the centrality of the Qurʾān to preaching and of the historical connection between storytelling and Qurʾānic exegesis.[17] The Muslim holy book naturally took center stage: surviving sermons from the medieval period, such as those of Ibn al-Jawzī, like virtually any religious text, are filled with Qurʾānic quotations. But the Qurʾān was equally important as a springboard of sorts, as presenting preachers and storytellers (and, for that matter, exegetes and others) with an opportunity to draw upon a host of extra-Qurʾānic material to fill in the gaps left by the holy book or to supplement its teachings. That in turn, however, suggests the difficulty of defining precise parameters for any particular category of religious discipline. It is a mistake, for example, to conceive of the *qiṣaṣ al-anbiyāʾ* literature as a discrete genre and one associated specifically and exclusively with storytellers operating on the margins of religious rectitude.[18] Stories of the pre-Islamic prophets make up a considerable portion of the standard exegeses of the Qurʾān transmitted and studied during the Middle Ages, such as those of al-Bayḍāwī or al-Zamakhsharī; it is significant that several of the major collections of the *qiṣaṣ al-anbiyāʾ* were compiled by scholars best known as Qurʾānic exegetes, such as al-Thaʿlabī and Ibn Kathīr. Stories about pre-Islamic figures were of course also recorded in the form of hadiths and as such can be found in the many collections of Prophetic sayings. The experiences of the pre-Islamic prophets represented an important episode in divine history, and so the earliest chapters of historical works that claimed to be universal, such as those of al-Ṭabarī and Ibn al-Athīr, recounted their stories; Ibn Kathīr's famous collection of the *qiṣaṣ al-anbiyāʾ*, for example, was drawn directly from the first volumes of his comprehensive history of the world, *al-Bidāya waʾl-nihāya.*[19]

Stories of the pre-Islamic prophets were certainly among the favorites of sessions presided over by popular preachers and storytellers. Ibn al-Jawzī indicated that among the best-loved topics of popular preaching circles were Moses and Joseph, and especially the latter's trouble with Potiphar's wife, identified in Islamic tradition by the name Zulaykha.[20] Such stories, drawn from both Jewish and Christian sources and sometimes known under the collective term *Isrāʾīliyyāt,* had of course been in circulation among Muslims from the very beginning, incorporated into the cultural and historical fabric of the new religious tradition by figures such as the converts Wahb b. Munabbih and Kaʿb al-Aḥbār, and as such lay close to the heart of Muslim religious discourse at all levels. The psychologically precarious situation in which the early Muslim community found itself, and the fragmented character of the Qurʾānic versions of biblical stories, which seem to presume knowledge of larger, more connected tales, encouraged Muslims to seek out other, perhaps older accounts of these stories.[21] The Isrāʾīliyyāt played an important role in informing Muslims about the scope and progress of pre-Islamic history—that is, of God's intervention in human affairs before the sending of the final revelation. Many Muslims accepted the proposition that the Jewish and Christian Scriptures contained accurate predictions of the appearance of Muḥammad and the triumph of his community.[22] Consequently, as Steven Wasserstrom has observed, the Isrāʾīliyyāt did not reflect only a nebulous and undisciplined stratum of popular culture; rather, they served a critical validating function, at least at first, attesting to the genuineness of the new religion.[23]

In time, as the Muslims came to define themselves in sharper opposition to the older monotheistic communities, many Muslim scholars grew suspicious of those who indulged in this extra-Qurʾānic material.[24] Ibn al-Jawzī's skeptical attitude toward such stories certainly contributed to his hostility to popular preachers and storytellers. His skepticism was shared by many, including the ninth/fifteenth-century historian al-Sakhāwī.[25] Nonetheless, use of the Isrāʾīliyyāt remained a common feature of Islamic religious discourse: even Ibn Taymiyya recognized at least some of them as an acceptable tool of Qurʾānic exegesis, at least under certain restricted conditions.[26] It is hardly surprising, therefore, that stories of the pre-Islamic prophets maintained their centrality within the tradition of popular preaching.

One of the channels through which the Isrāʾīliyyāt was accepted was that of the so-called *ḥadīth qudsī,* hadiths that take the form of direct statements from God, rather than the Prophet.[27] Such reports were by no means on the fringes of the Islamic tradition: they appear routinely in virtually all of the major compendia of traditions, and are particularly prominent in Aḥmad b. Ḥanbal's *Musnad.* Indeed, William Graham has remarked, in his study of the *ḥadīth qudsī* and their place in the early Islamic religious consciousness, that, if Mālik b. Anas's early collection of traditions, the *Muwaṭṭaʾ,* "can be said to represent the tradition of Medinan jurists, the *Musnad* might well represent that of the folk-preachers (*quṣṣāṣ*) of the streets and marketplaces of dozens of Islamic cities."[28]

What about the content of stories transmitted and sermons preached in popular circles? Here generalization is especially dangerous because of the paucity of sources that record directly the proceedings of any gathering. Nonetheless, from various sources, such as Ibn Taymiyya's compilation of hadiths favored by the *quṣṣāṣ,* al-Ḥurayfīsh's anthology of sermons, and the eclectic collection of stories and homilies in B.L. Or. 7528, we can at least identify certain themes and patterns of discourse which were common in popular preaching and storytelling circles.

Given the sparse and scattered Qurʾānic accounts of creation, it is hardly surprising that popular preachers and storytellers should satisfy their audiences' curiosity about the creation of the world and the theological meaning of the natural order. "I was a treasure," went a *ḥadīth qudsī* popular with the *quṣṣāṣ,* "but unknown; I desired to be known, and so created creatures, and taught them about me, and they knew me."[29] B.L. Or. 7528 includes a short homily on verse 260 of *sūra* 2 of the Qurʾān: "And when Abraham said, 'Lord, show me how you give life to the dead,' He said, 'What, do you not believe?' [Abraham] said, 'Yes, but [I ask] so as to put my heart at ease.' He said, 'Take four of the birds and make them turn to you. Put a portion of them on each hill, and call to them, and they will come to you in haste.'" The standard exegetical tradition identified the four birds variously as a cock, a peacock, a raven (or crane), and an eagle (or pigeon). Drawing upon that tradition, the preacher whose words stand behind B.L. Or. 7528 interpreted each bird as representing one of the four elements (*ṭabāʾiʿ*), both of nature and of the human soul—the raven, for example, is an "air bird" (*hawāʾī*) and represents lust (*hawā*) in the human soul. A Muslim must overcome these elements if he is to draw close to God, just as Abraham slew the four birds. But God restored the four birds/elements to life, and in that is a "great secret" (*sirr ʿaẓīm*): the elements in oneself are like death, but if one uses them in obedience to God, one may become, like Abraham, a true friend (*khalīl*) of God. This account follows the standard interpretation of the Qurʾānic verse—with the exception that one of the birds is identified not as an eagle but as a duck.[30]

Simple historical allusions provided some popular preachers with the opportunity to make bold cosmogonic statements. B.L. Or. 7528, for example, records a homily about the "rightly guided" successors of Muḥammad which links them to the cosmic order. That they numbered four, it says, reflects God's own exaltation of four pre-Islamic prophets in *sūra* 3, verse 33, of the Qurʾān: "God chose Adam and Noah and the family of Abraham and the family of ʿImrān above all others." Their number parallels the fact that man is made up of four elements: blood, phlegm, and the "two galls" (*al-mirratān*). If one of the elements is disproportionate to the others, the individual may become ill and die; so, too, if a Muslim does not love one of the four chosen companions, he may participate in the destruction of religion (a barb directed presumably at the Shīʿīs). Although the reception and understanding of such stories by their audiences are impossible to recover, some of them express remarkably sophisticated ideas. For example, another cosmogonic story was reported in the form of a hadith: "When God created reason [*al-ʿaql*], he said to it: 'Come here,' and it came. God said to it: 'Go away,' and it went away. God said: 'My glow and my splendor, I have not created anything more noble [*ashraf*] than you, and through you I take and through you I give."[31] This tradition, said Ibn Taymiyya, is false: those who transmit it—he specifically mentioned the philosophical school of the Muʿtazila—do so in order to elevate the status of human reason (*ʿaql al-insān*) to that of the "active intellect" (*al-ʿaql al-faʿʿāl*).

A related question concerned the place of prophecy in the divine plan and, in particular, Muḥammad's role in the prophetic order. "I was a prophet," he is quoted as saying, "when Adam was between the water and clay, and I was a prophet when Adam was neither water nor clay."[32] The term *prophet*, of course, was understood in a very broad sense by the Islamic tradition, and embraced figures such as Adam, Abraham, Joseph, Moses, David, Solomon, Jesus and his disciples, and others who, in strict biblical terms, were not "prophets." But Muslims viewed all of them as individuals sent by God to warn humanity, and they naturally served an important role in a tradition designed to "admonish" (*waʿẓ*) the faithful. In Ibn Taymiyya's collection of hadiths popular with the *quṣṣāṣ*, the focus tends to be on Abraham, reflecting perhaps the Qurʾān's own concern with a figure whom the Islamic tradition often identified as the first Muslim. "If Abraham is mentioned and I am mentioned, pray for him and then pray for me; [but] if I am mentioned and prophets other than Abraham are mentioned, [in that case] pray for me and then pray for them," the storytellers quoted Muḥammad as saying—much to the consternation of Ibn Taymiyya, who considered the hadith false.[33] Abraham's near-sacrifice of his son—in most Islamic versions, of course, Ishmael rather than Isaac[34]—was a moment of religious drama pregnant with meaning, and so was bound to be popular with preachers and their audiences. The preacher whose homilies are recorded in B.L. Or. 7528 responded to an audience perplexed by Abraham's anguish and the apparent cruelty of God's request. To extinguish their concerns he sought to give a "satisfactory answer which would put an end to obscurity, and calm [troubled] spirits, and free the hearts of the listeners of doubt and phantoms." God was simply testing Abraham's devotion, making clear to him that He sought his undivided attention. God desires his servants and his "friends" (*awliyā'*) to be preoccupied with Him only, and so heaps upon them trials and tribulations to remind them to focus their attention on Him alone.[35] As such an account implies, audiences were already familiar with the tales of the prophets, and so demanded of their preachers answers to questions both profound and playful. Since it is well known that the prophet Joseph's beauty and intelligence were priceless, how was it possible that his brothers sold him for a paltry price?[36] Why was it that Abraham, after his testing, sacrificed a ram and not a cow or a camel?[37]

More common among popular preaching circles were stories about the Prophet Muḥammad and his companions, as might be expected. A number of hadiths recited by the storytellers had a didactic purpose: "He [Muḥammad] stretched out his legs in a mosque, and God revealed to him: 'O Muḥammad! You are no longer in the dwelling of 'Ā'isha.'"[38] Others had less apparent connection to moral imperatives: "The Prophet said to Salmān [al-Fārsī] while he was eating grapes: 'Eat grapes two at a time.'"[39] Ibn Taymiyya's collection includes the predictable traditions praising the Prophet's closest companions, especially those who became after his death the four rightly guided caliphs of Sunni history.[40] Interestingly, however, the pious and stern caliph 'Umar b. al-Khaṭṭāb, whose reign was marked by a tightening of the moral strictures and behavioral guidelines by which Muslims were required to live, does not fare well in the particular hadiths excerpted in his anthology. In one, he is presented as a parricide—slanderously, said Ibn Taymiyya—while in another he is quoted as saying that, when the Prophet spoke with Abū Bakr, he ('Umar) would be "like the Zanjī [African slave] who did not understand," a tradition that Ibn Taymiyya considered a "plain lie."[41]

Quite a few of the hadiths in Ibn Taymiyya's collection present anecdotes that depict common or predictable incidents of daily life or convey commonsense advice consonant with the ancient Near Eastern tradition of wisdom literature, such as that reflected in the biblical book of Proverbs. Listeners were urged to honor the elderly among them as well as mothers and riding animals.[42] The collection contains a number of traditions that speak to matters of the heart. "Whoever marries a woman for her money," said the Prophet, "God will deny him both her money and her beauty."[43] One tradition, which Ibn Taymiyya observed in fact reflected a Qur'ānic injunction, urged the pious man to marry poor women so that in return he might be enriched by God.[44] "The bed of the celibate is fire," warned one, while another expressed the opinion that "a man without a woman is miserable, as is a woman without a man," words that Ibn Taymiyya observed could not be ascribed to the Prophet,[45] although they were fully consonant with the usual Islamic suspicion of celibacy. More practically, the Prophet "ordered women to flirt with their husbands during intercourse."[46] On a different level altogether the storytellers quoted a hadith that stated that "Egypt is the quiver of God [*kinānat allāh*] on earth: no enemy seeks it but God destroys him," the popularity of which surely reflected the prominence of Egypt in the political order of Ibn Taymiyya's day.[47]

Two themes in particular stand out as especially popular with storytellers and their audiences. The first of those themes is poverty (*al-faqr*) and a renunciation of worldly goods and powers. "Love of the world [*al-dunyā*]," went a popular hadith, "is the root of every sin."[48] Voluntary poverty and the shunning of secular distractions were, of course, important components of medieval Sufism—Sufis, after all, were often referred to as "the poor" (*al-fuqarāʾ*)—and we will return shortly to the connection between Sufism and popular preaching. But it is difficult to resist the temptation to understand the apparent popularity of traditions such as "your poor are [the occasion for] your acts of charity" (*fuqarāʾukum ḥasanātukum*)[49] against the broader background of the relative deprivation and inescapable uncertainty that were surely the condition of many members of a medieval, and especially urban, audience. So, according to Ibn Taymiyya, the storytellers assured those who fed the hungry that they were guaranteed a place in heaven.[50] A prophet who declared that "poverty is my glory, and in it I take pride"[51] must have exercised a compelling attraction for Muslims for whom indigence was a pervasive reality or omnipresent threat. Shuʿayb al-Ḥurayfīsh elucidated for his audience the saying that "the poor man is doctor of the sick, and his bleacher": if a rich man is ill and gives alms and a poor man prays for him, he will be cured; and, if a rich man gives alms to the poor and the poor man prays for him, the rich man will be cleansed of his sins.[52] And, beyond the consolation that comes with a shared sense of suffering, there lay the promise of recompense, if not retribution. The storytellers lie and contradict the Qurʾān, the *sunna,* and the consensus of the scholars, said Ibn Taymiyya, when they claim that God will inform the *fuqarāʾ* on the Day of Judgment: "I did not withhold the world from you because of your insignificance to me; rather, I wished to increase your power on this day. Hurry to the place of judgment, and whoever gave you a slice of bread, or a drink of water, or a piece of cloth, him you may hurry along to paradise."[53]

This in turn points to the last, and overwhelming, theme of the storytellers and preachers: that of death, judgment, and salvation. The certain threat of judgment led popular preachers, such as the individual whose homilies and tales are collected in B.L. Or. 7528, to dwell at great length on the wideness of God's mercy. In a story typical of those found in that collection, a woman gave her child a cup and sent him out to fetch some water. In the street the boy found youths playing a game, stopped to cavort with them, and so returned home in the evening without the water. The youth responded to his mother's queries with the comment that she should be grateful he had brought the cup back in one piece, and she in her love forgave him. The manuscript then records the preacher's exegesis of the tale. The believer is like the wayward boy: God puts into his hand the "cup of faith" and orders him to fill it with the "water of obedience." The believer, however, becomes distracted by the "games of the world." At the end of his life the believer is asked by God, "Where are your good deeds?" And when the believer responds that, despite his sins, he has at least escaped with the cup of faith intact, God writes in the "book of pardon": "I have forgiven you even before you asked for pardon."[54] This tale is typical of others in the collection also in its emphasis on personal salvation: by and large the doubts and fears of the preacher's audience focused on the fate of their own souls, rather than that of the community.

Such existential angst was reinforced by an expectation of the imminence of judgment which was not purely rhetorical. There is, of course, a strong apocalyptic strand in Islamic thought, and it is present in the storytellers' hadiths collected by Ibn Taymiyya. It is difficult to imagine why a tradition such as "Do not abhor the times of trial [*fitan*], for in them is the winnowing of the hypocrites [*munāfiq īn*],"[55] with its allusion to the political disturbances of the early decades of Islamic history, would be so popular with late medieval storytellers and their audiences, unless they themselves suspected the imminent arrival of an era of convulsion. "There will come to my community," the Prophet was quoted as saying, "a time in which the only one who will be safe in his religion is he who flees from lofty point to lofty point."[56] An imaginative listener might well discern his own predicament in such a prediction, but many would no doubt take greater solace from a favorable comparison to the respected companions of the Prophet. "At the end of time, the reward of one of them will be like that of seventy of you," Muḥammad told his companions. They asked him, "Seventy of us or of them?" The Prophet replied, "Of you, since you have assistants in doing good, and they do not."[57]

A strict jurist such as Ibn Taymiyya was no doubt disturbed by the tendency of the storytellers' hadith to provide shortcuts around some of the demands of the Sharīʿa or to promise salvation to Muslims on relatively easy terms. For example, the assertion that "Friday is the *ḥajj* of the poor" recalls the suggestion of, among others, the mystic al-Ḥallāj (d. 309/922), who was crucified for his controversial statement that Muslims unable to perform the pilgrimage could substitute local ceremonies.[58] Ibn Taymiyya reassured those who found inspiration in the alleged words of the Prophet that "even if the world were raw blood"—and therefore, according to Islamic law, unclean—"the believer's taking nourishment from it would be allowed [*ḥalāl*]," that God always provides the believer with what he needs and does not require of His creatures that which is impossible,[59] but an attentive listener might well find a more liberal license in the storyteller's hadith itself. Ibn Taymiyya objected to the claim that "Whoever eats with one who is forgiven is himself forgiven," because the hadith lacked a proper *isnād* but also because its message was completely wrong, since, he reasoned, infidels and hypocrites might by chance eat with believing Muslims.[60] On the other hand, assertions such as "Whoever lights a lamp in a mosque, the angels and the bearers of [God's] throne will not cease to pray for his forgiveness as long as the light of his lamp illuminates the mosque"[61] recall standard expressions of popular Muslim piety, such as the belief that prayers during the month of Ramaḍān or on the night of Muḥammad's ascension to heaven or in the Prophet's mosque in Medina are worth scores or even hundreds of prayers on normal occasions and in less exalted locations.

If any theme were central to the tradition of popular preaching in the medieval Islamic world, it was surely that of suffering (i.e., the suffering that we experience in this world), death, repentance, and the promise of salvation. The root meaning of the verb *waʿaẓa,* after all, is "to admonish," "to warn." Modern audiences perhaps require a reminder that suffering, hardship, and the capricious visitation of death were inescapable facets of the premodern human experience and so inevitably shaped religious responses to that experience.[62] The truism that the Islamic tradition is more world embracing than is the Christian misleads us if we allow it to obscure the approbation of the renunciation of worldly pleasure and the fixation on death and judgment which undergird many expressions of

Muslim piety. At one level this tendency gave rise to a strong tradition of asceticism and Sufism.[63] In more general terms it found expression in popular preaching. Meditation upon the misery to which humans are subjected in life, the horrors of death, and the promise of release to those who are God fearing was a staple of medieval sermonizing. Such themes predominate in the sermon delivered by Abu Zayd in al-Ḥarīrī's burlesque *Maqāmāt,* a caricature that is arguably all the more representative for its satirical nature.[64] Moreover, they infuse the collections of formal sermons which have survived, such as those of Ibn Nubāta and Ibn al-Jawzī. Ibn Nubāta preached *jihād,* but he also dwelt at length upon disease and death, the uncertainty of this life, the resurrection, and the world to come. Ibn al-Jawzī intended his collection *al-Yāqūta fi'l-waʿẓ* to be a "model" (*namūdhaj*) for preachers; the very first section of that work extols weeping and crying for one's sins. To make his point Ibn al-Jawzī drew upon hadiths, the example of pious Muslims such as Ḥasan al-Basrī, and above all stories about the pre-Islamic prophets, such as Noah, who wept for three hundred years after being censured by God and who was called "Nūḥ" because he was a "mourner" (*nawwāḥ*), and David, who never consumed a drink without mixing it with his own tears.[65]

Among individuals who were arguably closer to the Muslim masses than exalted preachers such as Ibn Nubāta or Ibn al-Jawzī, the theme of suffering, death, and eschatological redemption became even more pronounced. The preacher whose homilies and tales are recorded in B.L. Or. 7528 reminded his audience that gold has no value until it has passed through the purifying fires of a goldsmith's furnace, so too the believer, who must pass through the "agony of poverty" (*ʿadhāb al-faqr*) and the "fire of diseases" (*nār al-amrāḍ*).[66] One of the most frequently encountered characters in that collection is the angel of death (*malak al-mawt*). The interrelated themes of suffering, death, and repentance dominate much of al-Ḥurayfīsh's collection. The tenth chapter, for example, is devoted to stories of the *bakkā'ūn min khashyat allāh,* "those who weep in fear of God," a phrase associated with Islamic ascetics and mystics from the very beginning.[67] Al-Ḥurayfīsh, like popular preachers and storytellers generally, drew heavily on tales of the pre-Islamic prophets, such as Adam, who, according to one tale, worshiped and wept on Jabal al-Hind for one hundred years in expiation for his sins,[68] and David, who, in al-Ḥurayfīsh's account, functions as a model of penitence.[69]

Adam and David were, of course, notable among the prophets for their transgressions, and the weeping extolled by al-Ḥurayfīsh functioned first and foremost as expiation for sin—hence, for example, his account of pious Muslims such as the proto-Sufi Ibrāhīm b. Adham (d. probably 161/777–78), who wept at the recollection of lost opportunities to fast, pray, and worship.[70] The tears of the pious were meant to deflect eschatological punishment: Muḥammad b. al-Munkadir (d. 130/747–84), when asked why he wiped his copious tears over his face and beard, responded that he had heard that the fires of hell would not touch those parts of the body covered by tears.[71] But the psychological framework underlying sermons and tales such as those told by al-Ḥurayfīsh assumes an acute awareness of the present reality, and not merely the eschatological possibility, of suffering and death. "My brothers," said the Shaykh, "there is no preacher like death" (*ikhwānī lā wāʿiẓ kaʾl-mawt*).[72] It is not merely hell but death itself which frightens. Al-Ḥurayfīsh records a tale about Jesus, who, at the insistence of the Banū Isrāʾīl, once called upon God to raise Shem, the son of Noah, from his tomb. The prophet emerged with white hair and beard, explaining that he had thought that Jesus' call announced the resurrection and that his hair had turned white from terror. Similar stories can be found in standard collections of tales such as those of al-Kisāʾī, al-Thaʿlabī, and Ibn Kathīr, but al-Ḥurayfīsh added a twist: Shem told the Banū Isrāʾīl that he had been dead for four thousand years but that "the bitterness of death [*marārat al-mawt*] has not left me."[73]

No doubt al-Ḥurayfīsh's audience tasted the bitterness of death in their own lives; if they did not, his preaching aimed to make it plain. "The agony of death comes in truth," proclaims the Qurʾān (*sūra* 50, v.19). Truly, said the *shaykh,* quoting the Prophet himself, "the agonies of death are worse than one thousand blows of the sword." The threat was by no means abstract: his audience would understand his words, he said, "after only a few days."[74] The cemeteries (which, at least in Cairo, provided the venue for much popular preaching) themselves bore witness to the "agony of death." Shaykh Shuʿayb quoted the Prophet as saying: "No one passes amongst the tombs but their inhabitants cry out, 'O careless one! If only you knew what we know: your skin and bones will dissolve as does ice in a fire!'"[75] The metaphors of bodily destruction became more graphic still. What audience would fail to be moved by the story of a soul who visited its tomb on several occasions shortly after its death and watched as the lifeless body oozed water, pus, and blood and finally succumbed to the indignity of being eaten by worms?[76]

Such themes gave a distinctly emotional cast to medieval preaching circles. Given the emphasis in his own sermons on death, disease, suffering, judgment, and punishment, perhaps Ibn al-Jawzī should not have been surprised at the excessive weeping that, he felt, distorted the true purpose of sermonizing.[77] As we have already seen, some preachers, or imposters posing as such, feigned tears in order to impress their audiences. What such behavior implies, however, is that the manipulation of listeners' emotions, even if prompted by genuine passion and zeal, was the unstated objective of a preacher. The potential power of a preacher over his audience is demonstrated in a story al-Ḥurayfīsh recounted about the famous early *wāʿiẓ* Manṣūr b. ʿAmmār. On a Friday in Ramaḍān, Manṣūr was preaching on the merits of fasting, but the attention of his audience drifted away—"it was as if he were striking his flint against deaf rocks." When he saw how unmoved his audience had grown, he suddenly berated them: "O people! Is there no one who weeps because of his faults? Is there no one who desires that God forgive him his sins?" His harangue caught their attention and pricked their consciences, and they all began to weep. One youth in particular approached the *shaykh,* who told him to repent, reminded him of God's mercy, and then ordered the Qurʾān reciter to chant a verse (*sūra* 42, v. 25: "He is the one who accepts repentance from his servants and forgives sins"). The youth was transported and shouted out in rapture and joy—and then, the story goes, fell down dead.[78] The power of preachers, if not always lethal, was nonetheless real. An individual such as Ibrāhīm b. Miʿḍād al-Jaʿbarī (d. 687/1288), who led a famous preaching circle in Cairo, was esteemed and remembered for his ability to control the emotional reactions of his audiences: if they were crying, he could make them laugh, and if they were laughing, he could move them to tears.[79]

Behind the emotional facade of preaching lay Sufism. On the one hand, there was a strong connection between the emphasis on death, suffering, sin, and judgment in the tradition of popular preaching and storytelling and the asceticism and renunciation of the world which occupied an important place in the Sufi hierarchy of values. On the other hand, the connection was less a function of any *peculiar* impulse within the mystical tradition (jurists, after all, might feel an equally strong urge to admonish and exhort their fellow Muslims) than it was a marker of how broadly and deeply Sufi ideas had penetrated and of how central Sufism was becoming to the experience of being a Muslim in the later Middle Period.[80] Despite early criticism of preachers by Sufis, the ranks of preachers came to be dominated by individuals identified in the sources as Sufis, such as the Baghdadi *wāʿiẓ* Abū'l-Ḥusayn b. al-Sammāk (d. 424/1033), who preached in the mosques of al-Manṣūr and al-Mahdī and "spoke in the manner of the Sufis."[81] The connection between Sufism and preaching is already apparent in Ibn al-Jawzī's *Kitāb al-quṣṣāṣ wa'l-mudhakkirīn;* its author himself, for all his vitriolic condemnation of certain Sufi beliefs and practices, nonetheless had ties to the mystics.[82] His critique of storytellers and preachers, as that of Sufis in others of his works (such as the well-known treatise *Talbīs Iblīs*), was directed not at preaching and mysticism themselves but, rather, at certain perceived excesses of those who engaged in them. Thus, for example, he condemned certain of Aḥmad al-Ghazālī's disturbing Sufi ideas (such as his defense of Iblīs and his insistence that "whoever does not learn his monotheism from Iblīs is a heretic"), while at the same time noting that al-Ghazālī was a popular preacher and that, as a result, his teachings had a considerable circulation in Baghdad, "even though it is a house of knowledge."[83] In Mamluk Egypt certain Sufi orders were especially committed to preaching, in particular the Shādhiliyya, which included among its number the famous preacher Ibn ʿAṭāʾ Allāh (d. 709/1309).[84] The Wafāʾīs, of course, constituted a branch of that order. Their connection to preaching was such that Aḥmad al-Bulqīnī (d. 865/1461), great-grandson of Sirāj al-Dīn ʿUmar al-Bulqīnī, who held appointments in various mosques to lead *mīʿād* sessions and as *khaṭīb,* was identified by his biographer as holding preaching sessions in a small *madrasa* next to his house "in the manner of the Banū'l-Wafāʾ" (*ʿalā ṭarīqat banī 'l-wafāʾ*).[85] Moreover, as we know, it was from among the Wafāʾīs that a vigorous defense of preaching and storytelling emerged.

The connection to Sufism contributed to the suspicion with which some scholars viewed a practice that, in and of itself, was perfectly laudable from a pious perspective. The Sufi emphasis on the love of God, for example, led some preachers to introduce into their sessions amorous or even frankly erotic poetry. Ibn al-Jawzī claimed to have heard a storyteller recite: "I embraced her, but afterward my soul still desired her; will she after the embrace draw near? I kissed her lips in order to satisfy my love, but my burning love grows the more."[86] The preacher or storyteller might intend a metaphorical interpretation of such verse, but could their audience be expected to appreciate the nuance?[87] More dangerous, perhaps, were the suspect teachings of the Sufi martyr al-Ḥallāj; the storytellers' ranks, observed Ibn al-Jawzī, included a number of his partisans.[88] The danger persisted throughout the Middle Period. The biographer of the Sufi *shaykh* and preacher al-Ḥurayfīsh commented that "he uttered things in the manner of the Ḥarafīsh [a somewhat obscure group of Sufi mendicants] of Egypt, words which led him to unbelief [*zandaqa*], for which we ask God to forgive him," without, unfortunately, informing us of the precise nature of al-Ḥurayfīsh's offense.[89] The jurist, exegete, and preacher Shams al-Dīn Muḥammad b. al-Labbān (d. 749/1349), who held the post of *khaṭīb* at the mosque of ʿAmr in al-Fusṭāṭ and who "talked to the people in the manner of the Shādhiliyya," infused his popular sermons with the ideas of the controversial Andalusian mystic Ibn ʿArabī. In the year 737/1336–37 he was accused of major errors (*ʿaẓāʾim*) in his preaching circle (one source refers to it as his *mīʿād*), asserting, for example, that it was not absolutely forbidden to prostrate oneself before idols and exalting his own *shaykh* Yāqūt al-ʿArsh over the companions of the Prophet.[90]

Such excesses and deviations from theological norms were troubling to jurists and others such as Ibn al-Jawzī, Zayn al-Dīn al-ʿIrāqī, and al-Suyūṭī and provided fuel for their polemical fires. Defenders of the storytellers and preachers, such as ʿAlī b. Wafāʾ, went to some lengths to distance themselves from such malfeasance. When al-ʿIrāqī accused the storytellers of making false claims about God and transmitting incorrect interpretations of His word, ʿAlī responded that those who in fact did such things were indeed reprehensible, "misleading" (*ḍullāl*), "criminal" (*ashqiyāʾ*), and "enemies of the pious friends of God" (*aʿdāʾ al-awliyāʾ al-atqiyāʾ*).[91] But, in the eyes of Zayn al-Dīn al-ʿIrāqī and others, what made the *quṣṣāṣ* and *wuʿʿāẓ* so disturbing was not only the persistence of the allegations of error but the social context in which storytelling and preaching occurred.

3 / The Social and Political Context of Preaching

Returning to his home in eastern Iran after performing the pilgrimage in the year 486/1093, a preacher named Ardashīr b. Manṣūr al-ʿAbbādī stopped in Baghdad and began to deliver sermons in the great Niẓāmiyya *madrasa* in that city. The sessions, which Abu Ḥāmid al-Ghazālī attended, were extremely popular. According to Ibn al-Jawzī, the number of attendees grew with each meeting, until the congregation filled the courtyard, the building's upper rooms, and its roof. Judging by their relative numbers, women apparently were even more strongly drawn to the *shaykh* than were men. Eventually, according to the historian, the number of attendees reached thirty thousand. Al-ʿAbbādī apparently commanded his audience through a profound dramatic sense, since his sermons were punctuated by long and effective silences: "this man," reported Ibn al-Jawzī, "was more silent than not." His power over his audience soon grew obvious. In response to his preaching, attendees would shout aloud; some abandoned their worldly occupations in order to take up the *shaykh*'s call to piety and pious action. Young men cut their hair and began to spend their days in mosques, or roamed through the city's streets spilling jugs of wine and smashing musical instruments.[1]

Al-ʿAbbādī drove his audience, or at least some members of it, to live a more pious life or to implement, sometimes violently, the injunctions of Islamic law. Other preachers were able to manipulate their audiences to more explicitly political ends. For example, a preacher named Abū ʿAbd Allāh Muḥammad b. Aḥmad al-Shīrāzī (d. 439/1047–48) came to Baghdad and there "spoke to the people in the language of exhortation [*lisān al-waʿẓ*]." Attracted by his reputation for asceticism—"seduced" (*iftatana*), said the biographer al-Khaṭīb al-Baghdādī—uncounted numbers attended his preaching sessions (although, after acquiring a certain degree of wealth, he abandoned his rags in favor of more splendid garments). With his following intact, he turned his attention to holy war (*ghazw*), to the frontier skirmishes that were intensifying in the early fifth/eleventh century. He assembled a large group of his followers outside the city, where they banged drums and set off to the north, toward the frontier. Some eventually lost their zeal, for they abandoned their march around the northern Mesopotamian city of Mosul, but Abū ʿAbd Allāh himself carried on, ultimately reaching Azerbaijan.[2]

Whatever their purposes, preachers such as these potentially exerted a considerable degree of power over their audiences. Ibn al-Jawzī recognized this, and understood that the root of the preachers' power lay in their exposure to and following among the common people. To complicate matters further, however, it should be remembered that power in preaching and storytelling circles flowed in both directions. Preaching was not a simple, didactic affair in which one individual, whatever his standing and reputation, delivered his message to a passive audience. Of course, the reaction of a congregation to a sermon delivered or a story recited some five, six, or seven centuries ago is the most fleeting aspect of the problem, at least from the standpoint of the texts on which the historian must rely, and consequently the most difficult facet of the social context of preaching to reconstruct. But our understanding of the phenomenon would be incomplete if we did not assume that those who listened to preachers and storytellers had minds of their own and somehow collectively expressed their own expectations of what they should be hearing.[3]

An audience, for example, might help to establish the contours of a preaching session through the questions they put to the preacher. The sixth/twelfth-century traveler Ibn Jubayr described several preaching sessions that he attended in Baghdad, including one in which the scholar presiding over the sessions was pelted with a barrage of questions to which he then proceeded to respond at length, and another in which Ibn al-Jawzī himself devoted the bulk of the session to answering questions from the congregation.[4] In the anonymous record of a preaching circle recorded in B.L. Or. 7528, one can detect clearly the outlines of the concerns of the preacher's audience. Not surprisingly, they were disturbed by the story of Abraham's near-sacrifice of his son and in particular why God had imposed on the prophet such an apparently cruel test, and so the preacher sought to give an answer that would "make the hearts of his listeners free of doubt and uncertainty."[5] They were a discriminating group, and their anxiety over reports that seemed to cast doubt on the extent of the prophets' faith and their unquestioning submission to the will of God forced their preacher to lengthy excursuses in which he tried to resolve their apparently anomalous behavior. It was known to them that God receives the souls of the prophets when they die; why, then, did Moses resist the angel of death whom God had sent to claim his soul, almost tearing out the heavenly being's eyes?[6] It is well established that David was free of major sins, that he was pious and smart, and that he had ninety-nine wives; why, then, did he covet the wife of his "brother," Uriah?[7]

From a broader perspective the common people were capable of influencing the consensus of the Muslim community about what was and was not legitimately Islamic.[8] They were capable, too, of expressing quite vociferously their opinion of one preacher or storyteller or another, as al-Suyūṭī discovered to his chagrin. Even ʿAlī b. Wafāʾ, the great defender of the popular storytellers, worried that individuals who preached correctly—that is, ordering that which was good and warning against evil behavior—risked destruction at the hands of the "rabble" (*raʿāʿ*).[9] A Ḥanbalī scholar and preacher named Aḥmad b. ʿAlī al-Shīshīnī (fl. late ninth/fifteenth century) "concerned himself with reading to the common people from works of exegesis and hadith" and "was in much demand among them for that." Later, however, after he had expressed in writing his approval of the sultan's efforts to raise an extraordinary tax, the people turned against him and "despised him for this and loosed their tongues in both verse and prose"; they even tried to kill him and burn down his house.[10] There exists no fury, it seems, like that of a congregation scorned.

Consequently, the fundamental issue surrounding preachers and storytellers was one of control: who was to control their activities, their words, and their messages, and how was such control to be exercised? This was already an issue at an early date, as witnessed by the Umayyad caliph Muʿāwiya's efforts to bring those involved in preaching and storytelling under the control of his government, as well as by the political uses to which his enemies put the practice of *qaṣaṣ*.[11] Thus, the issue of control forms the subject of several important reports about the origin of the practice of storytelling. We have already encountered the hadith asserting that "only three kinds of persons narrate stories: one who commands [*amīr*], someone specially commissioned for that purpose [*maʾmūr*], or a hypocrite [*murāʾī*]," as well as the various stories about early storytellers, such as Tamīm al-Dārī, seeking the permission of the caliph to practice their art.

Ibn al-Jawzī, commenting on the hadith, defined *amīr* as "the ones on whom rests the responsibility for giving the *khuṭba,* and so they exhort the people and admonish them."[12]

What we are encountering here is the complex of issues surrounding the fact that Islam, unlike, say, the Roman Catholic Church, has no specific institutional structure for settling controversies of an ideological or doctrinal nature. This is a point that has been recognized for some time, and, despite the perhaps natural tendency of Western scholars to fall back upon unfortunate terms such as *orthodoxy* and *heresy,* it is one that seems to be relatively well settled.[13] On the other hand, the absence of a formally constituted decision-making body does not mean that it is fruitless to attempt to define an Islamic tradition or that that tradition has not experienced the necessity of setting, or attempting to set, boundaries to what constitutes permissible thought and behavior. Islamic rulers have been capable of instituting very precise limits to the theological positions that could be publicly expounded, as during the third/ninth-century *miḥna* (sometimes translated as "inquisition") set in motion by the ʿAbbāsid caliph al-Maʾmūn.[14] Less formally, the doctrine of "consensus" (*ijmāʿ*) has given the ulama an instrument, however unwieldy, which can be used to define what is and is not acceptable, particularly in the area of ritual and behavior. But, inevitably, the process of defining what is Islamic has been a flexible one, and one subject to a variety of internal and external pressures.[15]

This was certainly the case in the city of Cairo under the Mamluks, the forum in which Zayn al-Dīn al-ʿIrāqī and ʿAlī b. Wafāʾ waged their polemic over the storytellers. The Mamluks were perfectly willing to intervene in religious matters when a dispute threatened directly to disrupt the social order or when doing so would strengthen their own political position. Sultan Qāyt Bāy (r. 872/1468–901/1496), for instance, stepped into the simmering controversy over the verse of the Sufi poet Ibn al-Fāriḍ, firmly aligning himself with those scholars who considered it religiously unobjectionable, when doing so enabled him to realign the power structure within the ulama hierarchy in such a way as to consolidate his own authority and that of his Mamluk supporters.[16] More generally, the Mamluk practice of building and endowing religious and academic institutions should be read in part as an effort to bring the ulama and the religious sphere under some degree of influence and control.

But the Mamluks had little interest in taking up the daunting task of systematically policing popular preachers and storytellers; neither, for that matter, had most previous governments in the Islamic Near East. Zayn al-Dīn al-ʿIrāqī objected that the storytellers of his day did not bother to seek the permission of those in a position to judge whether or not they were sufficiently trained and knowledgeable to practice their art—in the absence of qualified rulers such as the "rightly guided caliphs" (*al-rashīdūn*), al-ʿIrāqī mentioned somewhat vaguely "those who govern" or "those who judge" (*al-ḥukkām*) and, more pointedly, the ulama themselves. In this they compared unfavorably even with Tamīm al-Dārī, who at least sought the permission of the caliph ʿUmar before he began to recite his stories. ʿAlī b. Wafāʾ responded that nothing in the report about Tamīm indicated that one is always *required* to seek the permission of those in authority in order to recite stories, only that Tamīm had once done so; perhaps, ʿAlī suggested, he had done so out of respect for the pious and esteemed caliph ʿUmar, as if to remind his interlocutor that, in political terms, the eighth century after the Hijra was very different from the first.[17] But ʿAlī also went beyond the formal question of permission. The hadith limiting storytelling (*al-qaṣaṣ*) to those who command (*al-amīr*) or who are granted permission (*al-maʾmūr*) was directed specifically, said ʿAlī, at the delivery of the formal Friday sermon (*khuṭbat al-jumʿa*), which, since it had an explicitly political purpose, was indeed to be delivered by those in authority (*al-umarāʾ*) or their substitutes (*nuwwāb*). Alternatively, he argued, the storyteller criticized in the tradition was one who did not "command the good and forbid the evil," or whose intentions in delivering his sermon were not pure. As long as the storytellers told tales that incline their listeners to that which is good and drive them away from the wicked, or which in some way "elucidate the book of God," in ʿAlī's opinion they had already been granted permission by God and His Prophet (*maʾmūr bi-dhālika min allāh wa rasūlihi*).[18]

Such license posed any number of dangers. Perhaps most important, it threatened to make the definition of what constituted legitimate religious knowledge far too open and uncritical, an issue to which the next chapter is devoted. It also opened the door to quacks and unscrupulous and venal profiteers such as those described, in different settings, by al-Jawbarī, Ibn Baydakīn al-Turkumānī, and Ibn al-Ḥājj. But the problem must also be seen against the background of the power wielded, or potentially wielded, by preachers and storytellers, because of their deep and privileged connections to the common people. Both Zayn al-Dīn al-ʿIrāqī and Ibn al-Jawzī understood the danger posed by the preachers and storytellers in social terms. According to a tradition cited by al-ʿIrāqī, and one that should perhaps be seen against the background of the broader concern that the Muslim community would share the unhappy fate of the earlier chosen peoples, the Banū Isrāʾīl had *quṣṣāṣ*, and this was a cause of their destruction.[19] He also recounted a tale about the first Umayyad caliph, Muʿāwiya, encountering and condemning a storyteller who preached without permission and then himself preaching a sermon suggesting that free-lance preaching had contributed to the hateful fissiparousness of the Jews and Christians. Could its consequences be any different for the Muslim community?[20]

All sermonizing took place in a social and even political context, but the connection between storytellers and preachers and the ruling order was problematic and fraught with tension. Preachers and storytellers could be a channel through which the ruling authorities cultivated the allegiance of the Muslim population or otherwise enforced their will. As George Makdisi has shown, preaching played an important role in the revival of Sunni power and the articulation of a more precisely defined Sunnism in Baghdad in the fifth/eleventh century.[21] Niẓām al-Mulk, vizier to the Saljūq sultans, personally invited several preachers associated with the Ashʿarī school of theological thought to preach in the Iraqi city, as part of his agenda of promoting Ashʿarism—even when the preachers' denunciation of the Ashʿarīs' enemies threatened the tranquility of the capital.[22] During the Crusades, too, Muslim rulers employed preachers to instill the spirit of *jihād* into their soldiers and subjects.[23] In a jurist and preacher such as ʿIzz al-Dīn al-Shīrāzī, an intimate of Saladin's uncle, Shīrkūh, who was also "brave" (*shujāʿan*) and who once actually engaged a Frankish knight in combat, the line between preaching and service to the state disappeared altogether.[24]

Such preaching worked to the advantage of the secular authorities, but possessed a power and momentum of its own, which at times threatened to spiral out of hand. In the early sixth/twelfth century, for example, a jurist named Ibn al-Khashshāb whipped an Aleppan crowd into a frenzy with his denunciations of the Franks for their profaning of Muslim shrines in Jerusalem and then, by way of revenge, led them in a march to convert several Christian churches into mosques by force.[25] Sermons preached on apparently theological topics could have profound political implications and could even inspire violence and rioting by those to whom they were addressed. This was especially true in medieval Baghdad, where the situation remained highly charged throughout the fifth/eleventh and early sixth/twelfth centuries, as the contours of medieval Sunnism were gradually established in the face of competition between, on the theological side, Ḥanbalī literalists and Ashʿarī and Muʿtazilī theologians and, on the political, the Būyid and Saljūq amirs and sultans and the residual and periodically resurgent ʿAbbāsid caliphs. A sermon preached there in 469/1077 by an Ashʿarī scholar condemning Ḥanbalī anthropomorphism set in motion a series of riots which lasted for five weeks. The situation became so highly charged that the caliph's council ordered the suspension of the activities of the *wuʿʿāẓ* generally.[26] This sequence of events was hardly isolated or unusual. In 521/1127 and again in 538/1143–44 the sermons of the prominent preacher Abūʾl-Futūḥ (or Abūʾl-Fatḥ) al-Isfarāʾinī in praise of Ashʿarī theology provoked the Ḥanbalī crowds and incited a series of civil disturbances (*fitan*), as a result of which the preacher was expelled from Baghdad.[27] As late as 555/1160, a preacher extolling Ashʿarī theology could be literally driven from his pulpit and threatened with death.[28]

The point is that preaching could, under certain conditions, have profound social and political ramifications, and so the practice was inevitably of some interest to those who ruled. As a result, some preachers drew their standing and influence from their close connection to those in authority. Such individuals were, of all possible types of preachers, perhaps the most likely to catch the eye of biographers such as Ibn al-Jawzī who both sought to record an accurate account of the leading men and women of their day and also hoped to help set standards for the preaching profession. For example, the son of Ardashīr al-ʿAbbādī, Abū Manṣūr al-Muẓaffar (d. 547/1152), an even more famous preacher than his father, whose sermons in Baghdad were widely attended, developed an especially close relationship with the caliph al-Muqtafī, whose trust extended to sending the preacher on diplomatic missions.[29] Given the tense but symbiotic ties that bound religious scholars and the ruling military elites together during the Middle Ages, it is not surprising that some preachers developed close relationships with the predominantly Turkish rulers and even profited from them. A *wāʿiẓ* named Zayn al-Dīn b. Najiya (d. 599/1202–3), for example, developed close ties to rulers such as Saladin and his sons, from whom he received "great wealth," which enabled him to fill his household with twenty slave girls, each worth a thousand *dīnārs,* and to dine in a manner befitting kings.[30] The Egyptian Aḥmad b. Muḥammad b. al-Qurdāḥ (d. 841/1438), a noted *wāʿiẓ,* musician, and student of astronomy, had the good graces of Mamluk sultans and the leading amirs, connections that allowed him to die a wealthy man.[31]

Other preachers, however, derived their reputations directly from their oppositional stand, from setting themselves against those in positions of power. Despite the formal connection between Friday sermons and political legitimacy, such opposition was quite natural to a preaching tradition that, as we have seen, stressed the ephemeral, even diseased, character of worldly success, wealth, and power and indeed forms a sort of trope of literary accounts of famous preachers.[32] What was required in a preacher was courage sufficient to preach a sermon capable of making the high and mighty weep, as Manṣūr b. ʿAmmār had done in preaching before Hārūn al-Rashīd. The famed Ḥanbalī mystic and preacher Ibn Samʿūn (d. 387/997), for example, ignored a prohibition on preaching promulgated by the Būyid amir ʿAḍud al-Dawla in an effort to suppress the communal violence between Ḥanbalīs and Shīʿīs which plagued Baghdad in the fourth/tenth century. Called before the amir, Ibn Samʿūn continued to preach and, according to a report recorded by Ibn al-Jawzī, moved the sovereign to tears.[33] The *wāʿiẓ* Abū Saʿd al-Muʿammar b. ʿAlī b. Abī Umāma (d. 506/1112–13), who had "a sharp mind and a Baghdadi intellect," was by all repute fearless in preaching to kings and princes, whether the caliph al-Mustaẓhir billāh or the famous vizier Niẓām al-Mulk. Once, according to Ibn al-Jawzī, he delivered a sermon to the latter in a mosque in Baghdad, addressing him directly as the "hireling of the Muslim community" (*ajīr al-umma*) and reminding him in no uncertain terms that his duty consisted in looking after the well-being of the Muslims and that God would demand of him an accounting of how he had discharged that responsibility. At its conclusion Niẓām al-Mulk was so moved to tears that he handed the preacher one hundred *dīnārs,* which he piously refused, instructing the vizier instead to distribute the money to the poor.[34] Just so, a preacher named Abū ʿUmar al-Ḥasan b. al-Filw (d. 426/1035) composed a poem in honor of himself and his preaching to an unnamed sultan:

> I went in to the sultan in the palace of his majesty in poverty—I did not make noise with horses or foot soldiers—And I said: 'Look! Between my poverty and your wealth is the distance between sainthood and separation [from God].'"[35]

Not every ruler was as pious and God-fearing as the sources portray Hārūn al-Rashīd or Niẓām al-Mulk, and by the Middle Period even Ibn al-Jawzī urged circumspection. Those who preach to sultans, he warned, should exercise extreme caution (*ghāyat al-taḥarruz*), for sultans reserve for themselves a monopoly on the use of force, and a sharp reprimand (*tawbīkh*) may appear to them as an intolerable public humiliation (*idhlāl*). Ibn al-Jawzī shared the common medieval attitude that manners and morals were in steep decline. Rulers such as Hārūn used to listen attentively to sermons, but now times have changed: rulers are arrogant, and corrupt ulama seek to flatter them. "In these times," said Ibn al-Jawzī, "it is preferable [for the honest preacher] to distance himself from such people, and to avoid preaching to them, for that is the safer approach." If a preacher is forced to speak before men of authority, he should take an indirect approach: he should preach by way of allusion (*ishāra*) or direct his remarks to the people generally (*ʿawāmm*), and mix his exhortation with statements about the nobility of rulership and remind his audience of the comportment of the just rulers of earlier days.[36]

Ibn al-Jawzī's personal circumstances—an enormously popular and well-respected preacher in sixth/twelfth-century Baghdad—made him especially aware of the complex nexus of preaching and power. Some members of the ulama no doubt played the sycophant to those who wielded the sword, but the rulers, too, were cognizant of the power of the preachers' word and so, he implies, feared it. Consequently, despite his warning, the ideal of the confrontational stance remained popular with preachers throughout the later Middle Period, and instances in which individuals lived up to the ideal were carefully noted by their biographers. In 638/1240 the famous preacher ʿIzz al-Dīn b. ʿAbd al-Salām al-Sulamī (d. 660/1262) quarreled with the Ayyūbid sultan of Damascus, al-Ṣāliḥ Ismāʿīl, over the latter's treaty with the Crusaders by which he surrendered to them a number of fortresses and the town of Ṣafad. To chastise the sultan for his cowardice in dealing with the infidel Franks, Ibn ʿAbd al-Salām refused to pray for him and dropped his name from the official Friday *khuṭba,* as a result of which al-Ṣāliḥ Ismāʿīl exiled the preacher to Cairo, where his nephew and rival al-Ṣāliḥ Ayyūb was happy to appoint the famous man to the pulpit of the mosque of ʿAmr.[37]

The Mamluk sultans and amirs provided the more intrepid among late-medieval preachers with ample opportunities to chastise those in power. ʿAbd al-Raḥmān b. Muḥammad b. al-Naqqāsh (d. 819/1416), a popular preacher who was appointed *khaṭīb* at the large congregational mosque of Ibn Ṭūlūn south of Cairo, was respected for "his severe and sharp ordering of the good and in his preaching [*waʿẓ*], both in his Friday sermons and his storytelling [*fī khuṭabihi wa-qaṣaṣihi*], so that he came to have high standing among both the elite and the common people"; more particularly, he was credited with a willingness to condemn whatever evildoing he witnessed or heard about, even if it embroiled him in controversy with the ruling Turkish authorities.[38] Shams al-Dīn Muhammad al-Dīrūṭī (d. 921/1515), a famous preacher at the end of the Mamluk period, was respected and feared, according to the Sufi biographer al-Shaʿrānī, by sultans and amirs, as well as by those of lesser station. Many of the leading figures of state attended his sessions; all left humbled.[39] Zakariyyā al-Anṣārī (d. 926/1520), by his own account, was fearless in preaching to the awesome but pious sultan Qāyt Bāy. "If I was unable to speak to him directly," he recalled, "I would give him my advice in a sermon, and he would grasp my meaning; and if I then greeted him at Friday prayers, he would come up to me to greet me and say: 'May God reward you for your faithful advice to us.'" The envious, he said, sought to turn the Sultan against him, and encouraged the Sultan to forbid al-Anṣārī from preaching to him in a disrespectful manner. But Qāyt Bāy responded: "What [would you have me] say to someone who has opened my eyes to my own faults and has given me good advice?" Summoning up all the rhetorical weight of the Islamic preaching tradition and applying it directly to the Mamluk system itself, al-Anṣārī was able to drive this sultan to tears:

> One day I said to him in a sermon: "Awake, O you whom God has put in charge of His servants, and think of your origins, and of your condition today. Once you did not exist, and now you do; once you were an unbeliever, and now you are a Muslim; once you were a slave, and now you are free; once you were ordered [*maʾmūr*^an^], and now you give orders [*amīr*^an^]; once you were an amir, and now you are a sultan. Do not accept these blessings with vainglory and pride, and [do not] forget your beginning and your end: for your nose will be ground in the dust when you die, and the worms will eat [you] and you will become dust." Then the Sultan wept and said to those amirs around him: "If I were to send this one away, who would preach me such a sermon [*waʿẓ*]?"[40]

Given the influence that preachers at least potentially wielded, the issue of control was especially problematic. Direct control, of course, was impossible, given the absence of a formal ecclesiastical structure. Further complicating the situation, as we have seen, much sermonizing and storytelling took place in settings that even the informal sinews of Islamic religious authority found it difficult or inexpedient to police, such as the great cemeteries outside Cairo. Moreover, many preachers and storytellers were peripatetics, traveling through the Islamic world, sometimes on pilgrimage, and practicing their art before always new and different audiences. Such wanderers already provided a stock character for al-Ḥarīrī's *Maqāmāt,* in which one tale describes the rascally hero Abū Zayd as appearing in "the equipment of pilgrimage" and preaching to the people of the Yemeni city of Sanʿa.[41] Not infrequently, such individuals acquired a good deal of contemporary fame: so, for example, al-Sayyid ʿAlī b. Yaʿlā (d. 527/1133), a famous preacher from Khurāsān, roamed through Iran and Iraq, receiving the enthusiastic approbation of the people (*wa ẓahara lahu 'l-qabūl al-tāmm min al-nās*), finally arriving in Baghdad, where he received the welcome of both the elite and the common people.[42] The Sufi preacher known as al-Shābb al-Tāʾib (d. 832/1429), who held *mīʿād* sessions "in the manner of the Shādhiliyya," circulated widely among the common people: he was born and educated in Cairo but visited Yemen, the Hijaz, Iraq, and Syria, most of them several times, and "constructed a number of *zāwiyas* in the various countries" in which to ply his trade.[43]

Given the fluidity of the situation, one can understand the bitterness of scholars such as al-Suyūṭī who perceived the power and influence of the preachers and storytellers and who worried that their discourses were not always, as it were, kosher. A treatise such as Ibn al-Jawzī's *Kitāb al-quṣṣāṣ* or Zayn al-Dīn al-ʿIrāqī's polemic against the storytellers was fundamentally an effort to assert control over what its author perceived to be a lawless activity or, perhaps more accurately, a cry of frustration that wicked and ignorant practitioners of the craft operated without any effective restraints. But in fact the predicament was not so stark as the scholars believed. The issue of authority and control, in relation to the activity of popular preachers and storytellers, was extraordinarily complex, as it was in all aspects of medieval Islamic religious life. There were at least sporadic, and not altogether unsuccessful, efforts to exert formal, if not systematic, control. More important, the preaching tradition itself set certain boundaries that prevented a degeneration into wholesale anarchy. Those boundaries were reinforced by the symbiotic, if sometimes tense, relationship between popular preaching and storytelling and the more disciplined transmission of religious knowledge represented by scholars such as Ibn al-Jawzī, al-ʿIrāqī, and al-Suyūṭī, and also by the thematic content of the preaching tradition itself.

The prospect of some form of direct control of preachers and storytellers by the ruling authorities was an old one, which at least in theory stretched back to the caliph ʿUmar's ambivalent attitude toward the *qāṣṣ* Tamīm al-Dārī. Al-Suyūṭī peppered his polemic against the storytellers with narratives from the early decades of Islamic history about the *ṣāḥib al-shurṭa* (indicating some high-ranking officer charged with policing responsibilities) taking action to prevent unauthorized *quṣṣāṣ* from practicing their art.[44] Those who dare to transmit false stories about the Prophet, he indicated, deserve to be whipped and threatened with even worse punishments; in these matters, said al-Suyūṭī, the ruler (*al-ḥākim*) should be appealed to for help.[45] Such arguments and anecdotes may be read most accurately as expressions of a pious hope and of the widespread pessimistic conviction that Muslim society no longer operated as it once had, and as it should, rather than as an accurate memory of a formerly consistent pattern. On occasion, however, rulers had complied, as when the caliph al-Muʿtaḍid ordered the storytellers (along with astrologers and diviners) swept from the streets of Baghdad in 279/982.[46] Several decades later the vizier Ibn al-Muslima ordered preachers and sermonizers, both *khuṭabāʾ* and *wuʿʿāẓ*, not to recite hadiths in their sermons without first checking their authenticity with the traditionist al-Khaṭīb al-Baghdādī.[47] In Baghdad in the sixth/twelfth century a caliph ordered a preacher expelled from the city after it became known that he "associated intimately with women, and perpetrated forbidden deeds."[48] The assertion by Ibn al-Ukhuwwa (d. 729/1329), in his manual of instruction for the *muḥtasib* (roughly, "market inspector"), that individuals who were not qualified should be forbidden to preach, and that those who did so anyway should be punished, would seem to indicate that this official appointee of the sultan held, at least formally, some right of supervision over the activities of preachers.[49]

It is difficult to determine whether medieval ruling authorities followed the advice of Ibn al-Ukhuwwa and al-Suyūṭī and systematically supervised the activities of popular storytellers and preachers, since routine matters often escaped the notice of chroniclers and biographers. Authority to regulate their activities was diffuse and shared by numerous individuals. Sultans, of course, held rights of appointment over preachers in the Friday congregational mosques, or at least some of them, and, when an official *khaṭīb* preached a sermon that challenged the political order, he could find himself dismissed, as Ibn ʿAbd al-Salām al-Sulamī discovered. But al-Qalqashandī noted in his eighth/fourteenth-century reference manual for scribes and bureaucrats that, in practice, the ruler's prerogatives were limited. He identified the official Friday preaching post (*khiṭāba*) as, "in truth, the most powerful [religious] post and most exalted in rank," since the Prophet himself had undertaken it. By his day, however, there were "countless" such positions all over Egypt, so that the sultan did not routinely concern himself with any but the most important, such as that in the congregational mosque in the Citadel of Cairo, or those in which, by the terms of their endowment, he held the right of supervision.[50]

Preachers in less visible positions must have been subject to even looser control. On the other hand, occasionally matters did reach a point where secular and/or religious authorities found it expedient to intervene, as did the Saljūq Sultan Masʿūd in forbidding ʿAlī b. al-Ḥusayn al-Ghaznawī (d. 551/1156) from preaching, after the latter began to incline toward Shīʿism.[51] Occasional anecdotes in the chronicles and biographical dictionaries give us some sense of how the mechanisms of control might operate. We have already encountered Ibrāhīm b. Miʿḍād al-Jaʿbarī, the charismatic seventh/thirteenth-century preacher who successfully manipulated the emotions of his audience. Writing several centuries after his death, the Sufi ʿAbd al-Wahhāb al-Shaʿrānī recounted a wonderful tale, according to which the qadis held a council in order to condemn al-Jaʿbarī's preaching and, in particular, his ungrammatical singing of the Qurʾān. After the council meeting, the Mālikī qadi issued a *fatwā* forbidding al-Jaʿbarī to preach but shortly thereafter fell from a gate of Cairo's citadel and broke his neck; chastened by this expression of God's judgment, the other qadis threw themselves at al-Jaʿbarī's feet and begged his forgiveness. Triumphant, the preacher told them that it was not he who had recited improperly but their ears that were at fault.[52] This story and a parallel one in which, after condemning the preacher, the leading ulama of Cairo suffered from the painful retention of urine clearly contain apocryphal elements, but the essence of the story is confirmed by the earlier and far more sober biographer, Tāj al-Dīn al-Subkī. He reports the council of qadis and their condemnation of al-Jaʿbarī, although in his account the accusing jurist fell, more prosaically, from his mule and broke his wrist, rather than his neck. He indicates that others, too, had condemned his preaching but that al-Jaʿbarī had persisted nonetheless and proved "his innocence and the correctness of his belief."[53]

What is of interest in both of these accounts is the interactive pattern of control and resistance: of a council of qadis and jurists seeking to restrain a popular and charismatic preacher of suspect convictions or dubious intellectual competence and his assertion of an independent right to preach. No doubt al-Jaʿbarī felt, as ʿAlī b. Wafāʾ might say, that he had been granted permission to preach by God and His Prophet.

Sometimes the qadis sought to involve the sultan in an effort to give their interdictions more force. Al-Shaʿrānī records another imaginative tale about Ḥusayn al-Jākī, a pious preacher who died in 730/1329–30, who, like al-Jaʿbarī, was accused of mispronouncing the Qurʾān. Again a council was held, this one presided over by the sultan, as a result of which al-Jākī was forbidden to preach. The *wāʿiẓ* complained to his *shaykh,* Ayyūb al-Kannās (the Sweeper), who arranged a trick. After the sultan had entered a toilet, Ayyūb appeared to him, emerging through a wall, with a broom in his hand. The sultan mistook him for a lion and, afraid that the cat was about to swallow him, fell down trembling. Ayyūb then ordered the sultan to issue an edict allowing al-Jākī to preach; the sultan having done so, the *shaykh* then slipped back through the wall.[54] The colorful ending of this story aside, its central drama—the qadis and sultan, in council, examining and condemning a popular preacher—was not unique. Ibn al-Labbān, who as we know was criticized for weaving monism and other suspect doctrines into his sermons, was condemned by the Shāfiʿī chief qadi Jalāl al-Dīn al-Qazwīnī and forbidden to preach at the insistence of a group of legal scholars, but not before the sultan and a group of amirs had become involved, the latter apparently interceding to seek his repentance.[55]

It would be wrong, however, to view the situation as one that uniformly pitted qadis and senior scholars, allied with sultans or other ruling authorities, representing a kind of quasi-official religious establishment, against more freewheeling preachers and storytellers catering to a popular constituency. There was considerable overlap between the different groups and the perspectives they represented. The various individuals of the Bulqīnī family, for example, ranked among the most accomplished and respected members of the learned elite of Cairo, but, in addition, they held their popular *mīʿād* sessions in mosques and *madrasas,* large and small, throughout the city. Here, too, the fundamental similarity of the material that formed the subject of class sessions, official Friday sermons, and popular preaching and storytelling is important. Tales of the prophets were to be found in rigorous and esteemed exegetical works as well as in more popular circles, and hadiths, of course, were a fundamental component of religious discourse at any level.

As a result, the storytelling and preaching tradition generated its own informal mechanisms of control, mechanisms built largely upon reputation and the moral force wielded by particularly respected preachers. Ṣalāḥ al-Dīn Muḥammad al-Kallāʾī (d. 801/1398), a Shādhilī Sufi, began his career as an official notary (*shāhid*) in a shop outside Bāb Zuwayla in Cairo but later became the companion of the *shaykh* and preacher Ḥusayn al-Khabbāz and in fact took up the latter's preaching duties in his *zāwiya* after his death.[56] Al-Kallāʾī seems not to have been a shining example of the preaching tradition: the sources report that he made glaring errors and carelessly mispronounced God's word and that his sermons contained misguided and unjustified exegeses of Qurʾānic texts. His errors came to the attention of the aged Sirāj al-Dīn al-Bulqīni, who took it upon himself to prohibit him from "speaking to the people" (*al-kalām ʿalā ʾl-nās*). In essence, al-Bulqīnī's reprimand was that of a widely admired scholar and preacher directed against an individual whose incompetence threatened to undermine the authority of all those who preached.

Practitioners of the art of preaching and storytelling might close ranks in order to silence a particularly dangerous individual. In response to Zayn al-Dīn al-ʿIrāqī's repetition of the tradition that "the storyteller can anticipate only God's wrath," ʿAlī b. Wafāʾ agreed—if, that is, the storyteller preached that which contradicted the *sharīʿa*. Such an individual should indeed worry about the retribution he will face on the Day of Judgment.[57] But in fact even the Wafāʾis did not rely entirely on conscience to ensure the integrity of their preaching. Take, for example, the case of ʿAbd al-Qādir b. Muḥammad al-Wafāʾī (d. 873/1469), a member of the order who originally trained to be a muezzin but who was drawn to preaching because of the "power, fame, and reputation" it brought him. ʿAbd al-Qādir, it seems, was something of an imposter, reciting poetry that he falsely claimed was his own and impersonating more famous scholars: once, while on the pilgrimage, he claimed to be Aḥmad al-Bulqīnī and led *mīʿād* sessions in his name. His ensuing altercation with Aḥmad, who, as we have seen, was described as having preached "in the manner of the Banū ʾl-Wafāʾ," seems in some way—the biographer al-Sakhāwī is sparse with details—to have led to a falling out between ʿAbd al-Qādir and the Wafāʾī order. As a result, some wags punned upon his *nisba* and labeled him "al-Jafāʾī," that is, "one who is alienated" or "one who is treated with distaste." The order, that is, took it upon itself to ostracize a member whose misdeeds embarrassed it in front of a family known for its concern for preaching and the transmission of knowledge to the common people.[58]

In the end the nature of the preaching tradition and the character of the sermons and tales that formed the bulk of the material transmitted in storytelling circles themselves acted to blunt the hard edge of the power potentially wielded by religious figures with close ties to the common people and to minimize the threat that they presented to the social and political order. Generalizations are dangerous, since we can know so little about the particular circumstances in which sermons and stories were recited and still less about the audiences' reaction to them, but the emphasis on the trials and tribulations of this world, and in particular on the promise of personal (as opposed to social) salvation, must surely in many instances have acted as a kind of social safety valve, deflecting and deflating the various pressures experienced by those medieval Muslim men and women who listened to the preachers and storytellers. The excessive weeping that disturbed Ibn al-Jawzī, and which was noted by many medieval observers of preachers and preaching circles, played the social role of internalizing the despair, anger, and angst of listeners. The suspicion of and hostility toward the world which were characteristic of sermons hardly amounted to a call to arms against those who benefited from the established social order. On the contrary, the spirit of penitence which sermons sought to induce, the copious weeping, and all the reminders of our frailty and sin and the hopelessness and injustice of the present world reminded listeners that true justice would be found only in eschatological time. Al-Ḥurayfīsh and his listeners drew comfort from the Prophet's observation that, of the eight doors to paradise, seven are reserved for the poor, while six of seven entrances to hell are set aside for the rich.[59] Social distinctions will be set aside at the end of time—God created heaven for those who obey Him, "even a black Ethiopian slave," and hell for those who do not, "even a Qurayshī *sharīf*"[60]—but in the meanwhile the underlying hierarchies went unchallenged. Ibn Abī Umāma preached fearlessly to Niẓām al-Mulk, so vigorously and forthrightly reminding him of his duties in this world and the punishment that threatened him in the next that the vizier, under the preacher's instructions, distributed a sum to the poor of Baghdad—but Niẓām al-Mulk remained vizier, of course, and the social and political order unchanged. In one of the few records we have of an actual medieval preaching circle, the preacher observed that on the Day of Judgment our lots in life will be reversed. Ascetics (*zuhhād*) and those who serve God (*ʿubbād*) will, in paradise, have plenty to eat and drink and live in large palaces and be served by houris, as do the profligate (*fujjār*) and dissolute (*fussāq*) in this world. By contrast, the profligate will, after the judgment, suffer the lot of those who scorn (or who are denied) the joys of this life: they will be poor, sad, and afflicted by trials and tribulations.[61]

Through mechanisms such as these, the social and even political power latent in the tradition of Islamic preaching, and in the ties that bound preachers to their audiences, was softened, its disruptive potential muted. This did not, however, mollify critics of popular preachers and storytellers. They remained alarmed over the mischief that, they worried, miscreant or undisciplined preachers might wreak on the faith and religious understanding of their listeners, an issue taken up in the following chapter.

4 / Storytelling, Preaching, and Knowledge

One of the most perplexing problems facing religious scholars in the medieval Islamic world was that of knowledge (*ʿilm*) and, more specifically, of defining what constituted legitimate religious knowledge and regulating its transmission. The importance of knowledge to the Islamic tradition cannot be overemphasized, since knowledge in effect defined the parameters of the tradition itself. In a sense it was knowledge that held together not only the faith but the world. With only a little hyperbole Ibn al-Ḥājj remarked that when a true scholar (*ʿālim,* "one who knows") dies, the whole of creation mourns his passing, even the birds in the sky and the fish in the seas. The question of what constituted knowledge was directly linked to the problem of authority—intellectual, social, and political—not only in the formal sense that scholars such as al-Māwardī (d. 450/1058), Badr al-Dīn b. Jamāʿa (d. 733/1333), and Ibn Taymiyya (d. 728/1328) constructed theoretical explications and justifications for the power wielded by caliphs and sultans, but also because knowledge defined the tradition that any Muslim regime defended or at least claimed to defend.[1]

That knowledge was found in texts, and so authority in the medieval Islamic world had a textual character. Authority was rooted in a particular text (the Qurʾān), and achieved its full dimensions in an immense and immensely complex tangle of commentaries on the holy book and other secondary texts that radiated outward from it. The power of the ulama as a social group reflected their ability to regulate access to and control of this community of texts. That power was not simply abstract: it was deeply rooted in social life, as Qurʾānic verses, invocation of Prophetic example, pious interjections, let alone the more or less widely known claims of Islamic law, reminded Muslims of the authority of that religious knowledge that was buried in texts, and so "directly and indirectly linked [the ulama] to what people took to be the sense of things, order in life."[2] On the other hand, their power had its limits. In the first place, of course, the absence of any sort of ecclesiastical structure led to a certain flexibility in the definition of *ʿilm*, a flexibility to which preachers and storytellers contributed and of which they were able to take full advantage.[3] Moreover, the tendency of the ulama to restrict authority to those who shared their training and outlook inevitably encouraged others to develop alternative models and mechanisms of religious authority, models that did not necessarily reject that of the ulama but which did nonetheless compete with it.

Since preachers and storytellers were in the business of transmitting religious knowledge to the common people, it was only natural that the question of knowledge should form one of the principal battlegrounds in the polemic over their activities. From the most general viewpoint their critics sought to portray the situation as one pitting legitimate versus illegitimate transmission and to define legitimacy in such a way as to call into question both the substance of the stories and other material they used and the manner of their transmission. Ibn al-Ḥājj, for example, tried to draw a clear line between a gathering devoted to the conveyance of authentic religious knowledge (*majlis al-ʿilm*) and that presided over by a storyteller (*majlis al-qaṣaṣ*).[4] Zayn al-Dīn al-ʿIrāqī, too, asserted the superiority of the *ḥalqat al-ʿilm,* in which participants "learn and teach" (*yataʿallamūna wa yuʿallimūna*), over what he referred to as *ḥalqat al-dhikr waʾl-tadhkīr,* whose members merely "recite the Qurʾān and call upon God," a distinction that his interlocutor, ʿAlī b. Wafāʾ, of course disputed.[5] It was legitimate religious knowledge that the storytellers and preachers transmitted, ʿAlī insisted, and if some attempted to teach that of which they lacked complete and certain knowledge, then the fault lay with those (i.e., the scholars) who taught them improperly in the first place.[6]

Given the nature of the material they transmitted, much of the controversy over preachers and storytellers inevitably focused on hadiths, which, of course, formed a critical component in the matrix of religious knowledge. The Prophetic traditions had engendered considerable discussion and disputation among Muslim scholars, who from an early time had sought to filter out those that genuinely descended from Muḥammad himself and to establish careful guidelines to ensure the accurate transmission of the traditions. Allegations that an individual transmitted unreliable hadiths or that he transmitted genuine hadiths without proper qualifications to do so formed a staple of polemic among scholars.

Storytellers and preachers, according to their critics, could not be trusted to adhere to proper conventions. Many who take up preaching and storytelling, said Ibn al-Jawzī, are "ignorant of [the procedures of] transmission" and simply "recite what they have found in books." Then, he said, "they address themselves to the common people, who are like beasts, and who cannot criticize what they [the storytellers] say. They recite and say: 'The scholar has said'; but the common people consider a scholar anyone who climbs the pulpit."[7] The passion and conviction that so clearly informed Ibn al-Jawzī's comments should not obscure from us, however, the reality that matters were rarely so cut and dry, that thoroughly reputable scholars could disagree about whether hadiths treansmitted by a *wāʿiẓ* in fact contravened the *sharīʿa* or whether they were transmitted in the full knowledge that they were spurious.[8]

The problem, according to the critics, was that the storytellers were bound to different standards than those of rigorous scholarship. "Most of the scourge of false hadiths are attributable to the storytellers," said al-Suyūṭī, "because they seek hadiths which soften the heart and are popular [with their audiences], whereas true [hadiths] are rarely like that" (*li-annahum yurīdūna aḥādīth turaqqiqu wa tanfuqu waʾl-ṣiḥāḥ taqillu fī hādhā*).[9] Ibn Taymiyya, in his compilation of hadiths popular with the *quṣṣāṣ,* provided an inventory of the traditions al-Suyūṭī had in mind. Most, although not all, of these hadiths he considered "invalid" (*bāṭil*) or "false" (*kādhib*), such as the reassuring statement that "whoever visits me and my father Ibrāhīm [i.e., visits the Prophet's grave in Medina and Abraham's in Hebron] in one year will enter paradise."[10] Some—for instance, the well-known hadith popular in Shīʿī circles in which Muḥammad is quoted as saying, "I am the city of knowledge, and ʿAlī is its door"—Ibn Taymiyya considered to rest upon "weak" (*ḍaʿīf*) chains of authorities, although they were included in many collections of traditions.[11] Others—for example, "Love of the world is the root of every sin"—Ibn Taymiyya claimed had no known *isnād* that would link them with the Prophet, although they could be traced to one or another of Muḥammad's companions.[12] Several traditions—"Whoever possesses useful knowledge and hides it from the Muslims, God will restrain him [on the Day of Judgment] with a bridle of fire"—were not accurate as transmitted, although their meaning corresponded to other hadiths that he considered genuine.[13] According to Zayn al-Dīn al-ʿIrāqī, whose criticism spurred ʿAlī b. Wafāʾ to compose his treatise in defense of the *quṣṣāṣ,* the storytellers, even those famous for their piety and probity, were known for their "weakness in reciting hadiths," mentioning a number of early transmitters such as Yazīd al-Raqāshī (d. 131/748–49).[14]

On the most basic level ʿAlī b. Wafāʾ challenged the assumption of al-ʿIrāqī and other critics that the storytellers were simply unqualified or reckless transmitters. No doubt there were some, such as al-Raqāshī, who were "weak [transmitters] of hadith," but their numbers also included respected figures such as the "rightly guided" caliphs and other honorable individuals charged with the task (*al-maʾmūrīn al-ʿudūl*).[15] In fact, however, the debate was far more complex than a simple matter of comparing the reputations of the various individuals who preached and recited stories to the community, and the response of ʿAlī b. Wafāʾ to the criticism of al-ʿIrāqī and others amounted to a vigorous assertion of the continuing openness and vitality of the concept of knowledge in Islam.

Scholars such as Ibn al-Jawzī, al-Suyūṭī, and al-ʿIrāqī objected to the fact that some preachers and storytellers transmitted hadiths that they had not learned through personal contact with a *shaykh* who was himself a recognized authority. As we have seen, it was such an incident that inspired al-Suyūṭī to compose *Taḥdhīr al-khawāṣṣ*. This objection, which was fundamentally formal and procedural, was nonetheless critical because it spoke directly to the criteria and standards that guaranteed the authenticity of the knowledge transmitted by the religious scholars. Those standards demanded that an individual who sought to teach or transmit a hadith, or in fact any other religious text, be linked to the author of the text, or the Prophet himself in the case of a hadith, through an uninterrupted chain of authorities (*sanad, isnād*), with each link indicating genuine personal contact between two individuals. So, said al-ʿIrāqī, "it is not permitted to any one of this description [i.e., a *qāṣṣ*, one reciting hadith] to transmit a hadith from books, even if it be one of the *Ṣaḥīḥs* [i.e., one of the two most respected collections of traditions, by al-Bukhārī (d. 256/870) and Muslim b. Ḥajjāj (d. 261/875)], which he has not read to one who has learned [it] directly from the scholars of hadith."[16] Ibn al-Ḥājj shared that concern. Individuals, he thought, "should not sit with a *qāṣṣ* or listen to the reading of books which are read without the presence of a shaykh to elucidate that which is difficult for the listener to understand."[17] The scholars' concern here was to safeguard the integrity of the system itself: therefore, a storyteller or preacher who is not properly trained but who even so transmits genuine hadith or who happens to teach some point of doctrine correctly nonetheless commits a "crime" if he "transmits that of which he has no direct knowledge" (*li-annahu yanqulu mā lā ʿilm lahu bihi*).[18] For such individuals "it is not permitted to rely upon books" (*lā yaḥillu lahu al-iʿtimād ʿalā ʾl-kutub*).[19]

When the hadiths or other texts transmitted were themselves false or in other ways dangerous, as was the case with the storyteller whom al-Suyūṭī challenged, the situation of course became that much more critical. The storytellers themselves were at risk: the first section of al-Suyūṭī's *Taḥdhīr al-khawāṣṣ* consists mostly of a series of traditions in which the Prophet warns that anyone who reports his words inaccurately, who lies about him, who adds to or detracts from his words, will be condemned to hell.[20] But so, too, were those who relied upon them for religious instruction: so, said al-Suyūṭī, the telling of false hadiths, such as the one that prompted his *fatwā,* was especially inappropriate "among the common people, and the rabble of the markets, and women" (*bayna ʾl-ʿawāmm waʾl-sūqa waʾl-nisāʾ*),[21] that is, those incapable, through incapacity or lack of training, of distinguishing the false from the true. All this was no laughing matter: as the Prophet himself had noted, "lying about me is not like lying about anyone else."[22] Al-Suyūṭī cited traditions predicting that at the end of time Antichrists *(dajjālūn)* would appear who recited false hadiths, and thereby seemed to suggest that things had degenerated so far that the end itself might be near.[23]

In fact, however, the situation was far more complex. ʿAlī b. Wafāʾ directly engaged the arguments of al-ʿIrāqī on the question of what constituted the authorized transmission of religious texts and traditions. In one respect he agreed with his interlocutor: the transmission by a legally capable person of that of which he has no direct knowledge is a lie (*ikhbār al-mukallaf bi-wuqūʿ mā lā yaʿlamu wuqūʿahu kadhib*). But his estimation of what constituted direct knowledge was considerably more liberal. If an individual knows a religiously significant story (*khabar*) in any lawful fashion (*bi-ṭarīq sharʿī*), or if he even *thinks* that he does, then he should be exonerated of the charge of false transmission, in ʿAlī's opinion. Individual storytellers and preachers, in other words, should be judged on the soundness of the material that formed their narratives and sermons. "Whoever speaks about the book [of God] and the *sunna* [of the Prophet] on the basis of what he has discovered about it, or what he has understood regarding the stipulations [of the law], or judgments which do not contradict the consensus of those whose opinion counts in such matters—there is no way he can be considered in error by virtue of his discussion [of these matters]" (*ammā man takallama fi'l-kitāb wa 'l-sunna bi-mā istanbaṭahu minhā aw fahimahu min al-aḥkām aw al-ḥikam al-lātī lā takhruqu ijmāʿ man yuʿ taddu bi-ijmāʿ ihi fa-hādhā lā sabīl ilā takhṭ īʾatihi bi-takallumihi*). Moreover, ʿAlī defended transmission on the basis of a personal reading of books, with a simple affirmation of the correctness of those from whom they are transmitted—"transmission from books when one is certain of the correctness of what was transmitted from them" (*al-riwāya ʿan al-kutub ʿinda 'l-wuthūq bi-ṣaḥḥat al-marwiyy ʿanha*)—rather than the careful recitation of the work transmitted in the presence of the author or other recognized authority. This mode of transmission, he observed, is known as *riwāyat al-wijāda;* it is one of the acceptable forms of transmission, albeit the least respectable. Nonetheless, he pointed out that many books of the religious sciences were transmitted in his day, and had been transmitted in the past, by just this method, and he insisted that most of the ulama were just as guilty of this lowering of standards as any storyteller.[24]

More important, the Islamic tradition itself generated a defense of the use of dubious reports, including those concerning the pre-Islamic prophets, against those who would set higher standards for their transmission. In the first place the conventions of transmission made a distinction between traditions that purported to quote Muḥammad directly and those that did not, such as those tales of the earlier prophets which were so popular among the preachers and storytellers. Al-Suyūṭī, quoting the seventh/thirteenth-century jurist al-Nawawī, concluded that "lying about the Prophet is forbidden without exception, whether in situations involving legal matters or in settings involving no strictly legal consequences, such as inciting, warning, and exhortation and such things—[lying in any of them] is forbidden, and among the gravest sins and most reprehensible deeds" (*lā farq fī taḥrīm al-kadhib ʿalayhi ṣallā allāh ʿalayhi wa sallam bayna mā kāna fi'l-aḥkām wa mā lā ḥukm fīhi ka'l-targhīb wa'l-tarhīb wa'l-mawāʿiẓ wa ghayra dhālika wa kulluhu ḥarām min akbar al-kabāʾir wa aqbaḥ al-qabāʾiḥ*).[25] He went on, however, to cite a hadith, traced back through the famous jurist al-Shāfiʿī, according to which the Prophet said: "Relate stories about the Banū Isrāʾīl, for there is no objection in that; but if you relate stories about me, do not lie about me [i.e., do not falsify my words]" (*ḥaddithū ʿan banī isrāʾīl wa lā ḥaraja wa ḥaddithū ʿannī wa lā takdhibū ʿalayya*). As the fourth/tenth-century hadith scholar Ibn ʿAdī explained: "If you relate hadiths from the Banū Isrāʾīl, transmit them as you heard them, whether they are true or not, for there is no objection in that; but you must not relate hadiths from the Prophet except with confidence [i.e., knowing that they are correct], for he has said: 'Whoever relates a hadith suspecting it is a lie is himself one of the liars.'"[26]

Moreover, as great an authority on hadith transmission as Ibn al-Ṣalāḥ (d. 643/1245) made a distinction between traditions that were spurious (*mawḍūʿ*) in themselves and those that, while suffering from defective chains of authority, and therefore unreliable, nonetheless might play a role in preaching and exhortation. "It is not permitted," he wrote, "to transmit a *mawḍūʿ* tradition to anyone, knowing that it is [*mawḍūʿ*], whatever its meaning, except to demonstrate its defectiveness, in contrast to other traditions with weak chains of transmitters [*al-aḥādīth al-ḍaʿīfa*], which [despite their weakness] convey truth in their meaning, which may be transmitted in exhortation [*fiʾl-targhīb*]."[27] Ibn al-Ṣalāḥ (and, according to al-Suyūṭī, later scholars including Sirāj al-Dīn al-Bulqīnī and Zayn al-Dīn al-ʿIrāqī himself) would go even further and permit a certain "tolerance" (*tasāhul*) in transmitting hadiths with weak chains of authority and those that "resemble the *mawḍūʿ*" (*mā sawā ʾl-mawḍūʿ*) but which are not in fact *mawḍūʿ*, except those that concerned the "attributes of God" (*ṣifāt allāh*) and the rules of the *sharīʿa* delineating that which is permissible (*ḥalāl*) and forbidden (*ḥarām*). In other words, the culture and conventions of transmission granted preachers and storytellers considerable leeway in "sermons and stories [*al-mawāʿiẓ wa ʾl-qiṣaṣ*] and extolling good deeds and other forms of incitement and warning [*al-targhīb waʾl-tarhīb*], and in everything which does not concern the law or matters of correct belief."[28]

Such rules gave the preachers and storytellers considerable scope. Here, again, the fact that few records of the proceedings of popular preaching and storytelling circles survive, let alone informative accounts of their audiences' reactions, limits what we can know. Some have suggested that the surviving works of an individual such as the famous Sufi and preacher Ibn ʿAṭāʾ Allāh, dealing as they do with complex theological issues and nuanced mystical insights, were not directed at "ordinary people" with "ordinary minds," that is, the sort who presumably attended sessions of the *quṣṣāṣ* and *wuʿʿāẓ*.[29] But we should be reluctant to dismiss offhand the intellectual quality of popular preaching circles, or at least the intellectual reach of those leading and participating in them. Certainly, the preachers' critics consistently worried that they dealt in intellectually challenging matters. Ibn al-Jawzī was adamant that preachers should avoid theological topics, especially those regarding God's attributes, for they were difficult matters on which even the ulama failed to agree and therefore utterly beyond the comprehension of, and thus dangerous to, the "ignorant common person" (*al-ʿāmmī ʾl-jāhil*).[30] Ibn al-Ḥājj, too, worried about the danger of reciting "problematic hadiths" (*al-aḥādīth al-mushkila*), such as that in which God was said to have created Adam "in his own image" (*ʿalā ṣūratihi*), to those who were weak in understanding, such as the common people and women: might they not fail to penetrate such a statement's "surface meaning" (*ẓāhirahā*) and so unwittingly be led to the error of anthropomorphizing God (*tashbīh*)?[31]

The persistence of their concern suggests that the problem would not go away. Ibn Taymiyya, as we have seen, reported that the storytellers popularized a hadith extolling the faculty of reason, one popular with the philosophical school of the Muʿtazilīs.[32] And a preacher such as al-Ḥurayfīsh did not shy away from quoting to his audience from such prominent and intellectually challenging Sufis as Abū Yazīd al-Bisṭāmī and al-Junayd.[33] Zayn al-Dīn al-ʿIrāqī complained that the storytellers spoke to the common people about things beyond their comprehension. Even if their exhortation was unobjectionable, they might lead their audience astray and unwittingly encourage "evil beliefs" (*sayyiʾ al-iʿtiqādāt*)—and how much worse if their discourse was itself false (*bāṭil*)? ʿAlī b. Wafāʾ, perhaps predictably, placed greater trust in the judgment of the preachers, relying upon them to recite "only that which would strengthen his [conviction] that his listener would understand that in which there is goodness and advantage" (*mā yuqawwī ʿindahu anna sāmiʿahu yafhamu minhu mā fīhi ṣalāḥ wa khayr*). As for those who *intend* to lead people astray, he said, we must simply seek refuge from them with God.[34]

In fact, popular preaching circles did at times at least touch upon suprisingly complicated theological problems. The anonymous record of one such circle, for example, indicates that the preacher put before his audience a question that had stirred great controversy among the Muʿtazilīs and their opponents—namely, whether a believer became an unbeliever (*kāfir*) by committing major sins (*kabāʾir*). The ensuing discussion did not rise to the highest level of sophistication but does suggest how a popular preacher and his audience might deal with complex issues. The Muʿtazilīs, he said, held that "through major sins, one leaves the faith but does not enter unbelief." The preacher first of all used the occasion to give his audience several possible etymologies of the term *Muʿtazilī*. According to the most common of them, the famous early ascetic Ḥasan al-Baṣrī expelled one of his followers, named Wāṣil, from his circle for arguing what became the Muʿtazilī position, that the sinning believer occupies an intermediate place between belief and unbelief, and so named the misguided one *muʿtazilī* (dissociated one) for his error.[35] More colorfully, the preacher added that the situation was like that of a man who does not wish to impregnate his concubine. During intercourse, when he feels ejaculation approaching, he withdraws his penis, an act known as *ʿazl* (from the same root as *muʿtazilī*), that is, to experience ejaculation outside the womb. In the same way, the preacher reasoned, Ḥasan expelled his wayward pupil before he completed his education.

The occasion led the preacher to discuss other tenets of the Muʿtazilī, the Qadarī, and other rationalist schools of thought. The Muʿtazila, for example, argue on the basis of the Qurʾānic verse "eyes do not reach him" (6.103) that no one will literally "see" God. Such reasoning is flawed, the preacher replied; the Qurʾān's words indicate only that *some* eyes—those of the true believers—will be privileged with the sight of God. He followed this line of thought with what can only be described as horse sense. If a man has a valuable jewel, he may not show it to everyone, especially those who desire it for themselves, but that does not mean that *no one* will see the jewel, for the owner may well choose to show it to others. The Muʿtazila, he reasoned, must be wrong to insist that God cannot be "seen," for that which is not seen is nonexistent (*maʿdūm*), and that which is nonexistent "cannot be the Necessarily Existent" (*lā yakūnu wājib al-wujūd*).

True to the preferences of the popular preaching tradition, the foregoing discussion provided this preacher with the opportunity to relate and discuss a story from the Isrāʾīliyyāt. God instructed Moses: "You will not see me [directly]; rather, look upon the mountain" (Qurʾān 7.143). When Moses did so, he saw the "light of Muḥammad," which was so powerful that it temporarily rendered him unconscious. When he descended the mountain, Gabriel came and warned him to cover his face, so that the reflected glory (of Muḥammad) would not blind those who looked upon him. First Moses tried a veil, but the radiance on his face was so strong that the veil was incinerated. So, in succession, were his turban and a piece of leather engulfed in flames. "My God," he exclaimed, "at this rate I shall burn up the entire Banū Isrāʾīl!" So Gabriel advised him to veil his face with a piece of the robe of a Sufi (*faqīr*) or scholar (*ʿālim*), and, in the event, no one was harmed. From this tale the preacher drew a simple moral: that on the day of Resurrection, sinners shall be saved from the fires of Hell by the knowledge of the ulama and prayers of the Sufis.[36]

Discussion by popular preachers of issues such as those raised by the Muʿtazila, even on a superficial level, fueled the concern of scholars such as Ibn Taymiyya and Zayn al-Dīn al-ʿIrāqī. The problem, however, was not simply a topical one, a disagreement over the scope of matters that could legitimately be addressed in popular preaching and storytelling circles. A more fundamental issue concerned the nature and limits of intellectual authority. The polemic between Zayn al-Dīn al-ʿIrāqī and ʿAlī b. Wafāʾ addressed this issue through a discussion of the third/ninth-century moralizer, preacher, and theologian al-Ḥārith b. Asad al-Muḥāsibī (whom Louis Massignon labeled "the most illustrious" of those identified as *quṣṣāṣ*) and his controversial legacy. Al-ʿIrāqī quoted al-Muḥāsibī's contemporary, the hadith scholar and student of Aḥmad b. Ḥanbal, Abū Zurʿa al-Rāzī, who, in response to a question, opined that al-Muḥāsibī's works contain "innovations and errors of evil influence, and you will find in them that which you can do without." In response to the observation that they nonetheless also contained good advice or a sound lesson (*ʿibra*), Abū Zurʿa contended that the *ʿibra* of the Qurʾān was sufficient. The problem again was one of intellectual competence, of the knowledge and discernment necessary to separate that which was true *and* safe, on the one hand, from that which was true but cloaked in the garb of subtlety and nuance. After all, respected scholars such as Mālik b. Anas (d. 179/796) and ʿAbd al-Rahmān al-Awzāʿī (d. 157/774) had written books containing "wicked suggestions and whispers" (*khaṭarāt wa wasāwis*) which, if not properly understood, might lead the "people" (*al-nās*) into unlawful innovation.[37]

For ʿAlī b. Wafāʾ the critical factor was that of *ʿibra*, by which he meant a "warning," "moral," or "lesson." The term *ʿibra* drew on the rich and ambivalent meanings of its underlying root, ʿ/b/r, which can mean, among other things, "to pass through, over, or beyond" and also "to pass from the outside to the inside of a thing." Consequently, *ʿibra* figured prominently in several layers of discourse within the Muslim literary tradition: philosophers used the term, as did historians such as Ibn Khaldūn, who employed it (in its plural form, *ʿibar*) prominently in the title of his great work of universal history.[38] The term is found in the Qurʾān, for example at the end of *Sūrat Yūsuf,* in which the stories of the prophets are identified as a "lesson" for those who would hear, or in the seventy-ninth *sūra,* in which it characterizes the story of Moses.[39] *ʿIbra* was a technical term in the Sufi vocabulary which indicated right guidance in matters concerning good and evil, the distinction between outward form and inward truth, and by extension how souls pass successfully from this world to paradise.[40]

ʿAlī drew on the rich layers of meaning embedded in the term and understood *ʿibra* to denote not merely advice but the quality of having absorbed, and being able to discern, true spiritual guidance. He did not contradict the words of Abū Zurʿa, who was, he acknowledged, one of the authoritative scholars (*al-aʾimma*) of the Islamic tradition. But he understood Abū Zurʿa to say that the dangerous works of al-Muḥāsibī and others mentioned "innovations" and "errors" in the course of warning against them, so that anyone with a "sound understanding" (*fahm salīm*) could safely read them. Perhaps, he speculated, Abū Zurʿa was of the opinion that the individual who submitted to him the question concerning al-Muḥāsibī's books did not possess the qualitites of mind and of character which would enable him to read them in safety. He noted that when someone objected that the works of al-Muḥāsibī did in fact contain sound and proper *ʿibra,* Abū Zurʿa did not deny it.[41]

The critical thing in all matters of religion was the quality and the sincerity of the *ʿibra.* "The truthfulness of the *ʿibra,*" said ʿAlī "is the means of passing from peril to salvation in every station" (*ḥaqīqat al-ʿibra sabab al-ʿubūr min al-mahlaka ilā ʾl-najāh fī kull maqām*). No doubt sufficient means of salvation are to be found in the Qurʾān, and, if one has not absorbed the *ʿibra* of the holy book, one will not find it in the works of al-Muḥāsibī. But the same, he observed, could be said of *all* books of a religious or legal character. ʿAlī's analysis reflects the Sufi concern with intention and inner understanding, but he goes on to enunciate a defense of honest disagreement, even regarding the interpretation of the textual foundations of the faith. "Whoever investigates [the matter] with a sound heart, with no distortion from one side or another," he wrote, "will realize what we said to you, God willing, that to understand the words of one Muslim concerning another [Muslim] in their best light is a matter [befitting] the pious. This is well known even among those who interpret the word of God and His Prophet but differ in opinion."[42]

But the problem was not limited to a discussion of previous writers and ancient controversies. On the contrary, both ʿAlī b. Wafāʾ and his interlocutors were forward looking and clashed over the broad parameters of what legitimate religious knowledge in Islam could entail. Here the dispute centered on dreams and visions and their suitability as a means of conveying knowledge. The problems posed by visions of the Prophet bedeviled Islamic authors throughout the Middle Period. ʿAlī b. Wafāʾ himself acknowledged that the issue was a "difficult problem" (*masʾala mushkila*) and one that demanded fuller treatment than he was prepared to give it in his defense of preachers and storytellers.[43] Nonetheless, the outline of the problem as it related to storytelling and preaching can be discerned fairly clearly.

In the first place most authorities agreed that the Prophet might well communicate with individuals from his community via dreams, a position that was widely accepted in Sufi circles.[44] For this there was ample support in the Prophetic traditions, as in Muḥammad's statement, as transmitted by Abū Hurayra and recorded by al-Bukhārī, that "whoever sees me in a dream will see me in his wakefulness, and Satan cannot imitate me in shape."[45] Jalāl al-Dīn al-Suyūṭī himself went further and defended, albeit cautiously, the possibility that some spiritually gifted individuals might actually see the Prophet "in wakefulness" (*fīʾl-yaqẓa*), arguing that those who denied the reality of such visions constituted "a group of people in this day who have no standing in knowledge."[46] Such visions were accepted because they were, in a literal sense, "real" or had the power to shape the reality of those who saw them. The Sufi preacher al-Ḥurayfīsh recounted a tale told by Abū ʿAbd Allāh Muḥammad b. al-Walāʾ about a visit he had made to the Prophet's tomb in Medina. Overcome by hunger, he fell asleep; while dreaming, he saw the Prophet, who gave him a loaf of bread, of which he ate half. Upon waking, Abū ʿAbd Allāh discovered the other half of the loaf in his hand.

More important, dreams and visions were closely related to the institution of prophecy in Islamic understanding. It is true that prophecy as a legislative project had come to a close with the career of Muḥammad; nonetheless, a portion of the prophetic link between God and mankind remained in the form of dreams.[47] "The sound dream [*al-ruʾyā ʾl-ṣāliḥa*] is one of the forty-six parts of prophecy," in the words of a tradition that, in different versions, is found scattered throughout the principal collections of hadith.[48] Indeed, the Prophetic vision could even prove to be a defense *against* the depredations of those who transmitted false religious information, as al-Suyūṭī acknowledged in reporting several instances of Muḥammad's appearing in a dream to warn that an individual was reciting hadith that did not reflect the Prophet's actual words.[49] In one instance an unnamed "saint" (*walī*) attended a session in which a jurist was reciting hadith and told the scholar that a tradition he had just repeated was false. "Who told you that?" inquired the scholar, to which the saint replied: "The Prophet is standing over your head, saying: 'I never said this hadith.'"[50]

Oneiromancy and the interpretation of dreams had, of course, long played an important role in Near Eastern societies, with a genealogy that extended back well beyond the Islamic period. In medieval Islamic culture, however, dreams also functioned as an important mode of legitimization for both individuals and particular points of view on a host of religious or legal subjects. So, for example, Islamic literature is replete with accounts of dreams, many of them featuring an appearance by the Prophet, which served to extol and affirm the legitimacy of the principal Sunni schools of law (*madhāhib*) and their eponyms.[51] On a more idiosyncratic level a somewhat odd ninth/fifteenth-century North African figure named Muḥammad al-Zawāwī recorded a series of visions of Muḥammad and other religious worthies through which he hoped to establish and confirm his own rather exalted opinion of himself.[52]

An interesting example of legitimization through dreams involved ʿAbd Allāh b. Saʿd b. Abī Jamra, a hadith scholar with a reputation for piety who died in Cairo in 675/1277.[53] Among the works he left to posterity is a "Book of Visions" (*Kitāb al-marāʾī*), in which he records a series of visions in which Muḥammad appeared to confirm the merits of Ibn Abī Jamra's commentary on al-Bukhārī's collection of hadith. A typical example of these visions recounted an episode in which Muḥammad appeared in Ibn Abī Jamra's home, along with his wives and companions, and began to peruse the scholar's commentary. Ibn Abī Jamra handed him the page including his gloss on Bukhārī's account of the *ḥadīth al-ifk,* the famous story of the slander against Muḥammad's wife, ʿĀʾisha. According to Ibn Abī Jamra, Muḥammad was pleased by this commentary, handed it to ʿĀʾisha, and ordered her to pray for the author.[54] This story, and others like it in the *Kitāb al-marāʾī,* is a perfect example of the dream as a tool of legitimization. But such visions remained a point of controversy. According to al-Shaʿrānī's account of Ibn Abī Jamra's life and career, when the scholar once publicly announced that he had seen and spoken with the Prophet "in wakefulness," a group of people (*baʿḍ al-nās*) attacked him, in response to which the reclusive scholar shut himself in his house, where he remained until his death.[55]

The use of dreams as a polemical tool, and the controversy that it engendered, related directly to the question of preaching and storytelling. Zayn al-Dīn al-ʿIrāqī acknowledged that Muḥammad had been reliably reported as saying that "no trace of prophethood remains except the sound dream [*al-ruʾyā ʾl-ṣāliḥa*]"; nonetheless, he worried that many people could be misled (*yaghtarru*) by dreams related by preachers and storytellers.[56] Others shared his concern that dreams featuring the Prophet might be fabricated, deliberately or unconsciously; their fears even resulted in a warning, expressed in a hadith and paralleling others speaking to the fabrication of Prophetic traditions, which condemned those falsely reporting their visions and dreams.[57] But for ʿAlī b. Wafāʾ, of course, the Prophet's words constituted a much broader license. Good news (*al-bushrā*) received by a reliable vision should be announced to the world, as the Prophet himself had commanded: "If one sees a good dream, let him spread the news" (*fa-in raʾā ruʾyā ḥasana fal-yubashshir*).[58]

A more particular problem concerned those storytellers and preachers who alleged that the Prophet himself communicated to them via dreams or visions his specific permission to speak—that is, to preach or tell stories—to the people. From al-ʿIrāqī's account it would appear that such claims were not unusual. The scholar, of course, took a skeptical view of such claims: Muḥammad did not, he reasoned, allow what he forbade, and these visions are not true and reliable. Once again, ʿAlī b. Wafāʾ sought to deflect the criticism by agreeing with it, if al-ʿIrāqī's criticism were directed at those who lie, who report falsely about God and His Prophet, and who would lead their listeners astray. But he denied his interlocutor's implication that storytelling itself was forbidden by the consensus (*ijmāʿ*) of the Islamic community: "It is credible that the Prophet of God might permit [i.e., in a dream] what the people of the consensus have not agreed is forbidden according to the law" (*yajūzu an yaʾdhana rasūl allāh fīmā lam yujmiʿ ahl al-ijmāʿ ʿalā annahu manhiy ʿanhu sharʿan*). More significantly, he would judge such preachers on an individual basis: if that which (they claimed) the Prophet revealed to them in a dream was "credible of occurrence from him" (*jāʾiz al-wuqūʿ minhu*)—that is, if it was consistent with and worthy of the Prophet—then it should be accepted as legitimate.[59]

Al-ʿIrāqī's skepticism amounted to a direct challenge to the authority of preachers such as ʿAlī b. Wafāʾ himself, and ʿAlī's defense of Prophetic inspiration as a source of legitimation must be understood in personal as well as general terms. A ninth/fifteenth-century account of the virtues and splendid deeds of the Wafāʾī *shaykhs* ascribed ʿAlī's own eloquence to the intervention of the Prophet in a vision. Already at the age of five, ʿAlī's tongue was loosed through Prophetic inspiration. One day, while studying with his Qurʾān teacher, and "while in a state of wakefulness, not in sleep" (*yaqẓat*^{an} *wa lā manām*^{an}), ʿAlī saw Muḥammad. Suddenly ʿAlī saw himself wearing the white cotton shirt that had until then been on the Prophet's back. The Prophet ordered him to recite—*iqraʾ,* the same command that Gabriel had spoken to Muḥammad in the cave outside Mecca—so he recited *Sūrat al-ḍuḥā* (*sūra* 93) and *Sūrat al-inshirāḥ* (94). But the connection between eloquence in preaching and a vision of the Prophet went deeper. "When I reached the age of twenty-one [ʿAlī is quoted as saying], I purified myself for morning prayers in the Qarāfa, when I saw the Prophet in front of my face. He embraced me and said: 'As for the blessings of your Lord, speak about them'" (Qurʾān 93.11). "From that point on," continued this account of his early life, "his tongue was loosened [*fa-utiyat lisānuhu min dhālika ʾl-waqt*]."[60]

In fact, such a claim was by no means outrageous. The famous and respected preacher Ibn Nubāta, for instance, alleged Muḥammad's approbation of his preaching in a dream. One night, he recounted, he dreamed that he was standing in a cemetery outside the city of Mayyāfāriqīn, when the Prophet appeared to him and said: "'O greatest of preachers [lit., "preacher of preachers," *khaṭīb al-khuṭabāʾ*], what do you say?' and he pointed to the tombs. And I replied: 'They do not tell of what has come to pass. Were they able to speak, they would do so, [but] they have drunk the bitter cup of death.'" Ibn Nubāta, drawing fully upon the conventions of his craft, then launched into a formal disquisition on the terrors of death and the final judgment, at the end of which the Prophet embraced him and spat in his mouth, signifying his approval. When he awoke, Ibn Nubāta recounted, he felt a happiness such as he had never experienced; a glow on his face and the smell of musk in his mouth seemed to confirm the preacher's account. Ibn Nubāta told (*qaṣṣa*) the story of this dream to the people and let them know that the Prophet had named him "preacher" (*khaṭīb*).[61]

The problem of inspiration via a dream vision of the Prophet spoke to broader issues concerning the contours of acceptable religious knowledge. The dream in which the Prophet or some other respected religious figure expressed approval of some individual or point of view was a staple of medieval Islamic literature and served as an important means of legitimation—in which function, in fact, it provided a remarkable parallel to hadith.[62] Al-ʿIrāqī worried that some storytellers might "see" the Prophet ordering that which was known to be forbidden or forbidding that which the law enjoined and then transmit that "knowledge" to the unsuspecting and undiscerning; as an illustration, he mentioned the killing of someone, the shedding of whose blood was not licit. Such a vision surely was a delusion (*takhayyul*). ʿAlī b. Wafāʾ could only agree—up to a point. An individual who claimed to have heard the Prophet enjoining that which was forbidden or forbidding what he had allowed had "erred in his hearing without a doubt" (*qad ghaliṭa fī masmūʿihi bi-lā shakk*). Messages received through visions that did *not* violate the consensus (*ijmāʿ*) of the scholars, however, must be considered correct (*ṣaḥīḥa*).[63]

That is potentially a radical position indeed. On one level ʿAlī b. Wafāʾ's arguments simply exploit the absence of any formal ecclesiastical structure in Islam to expand the circle of those recognized as competent to contribute to the consensus of the community. On a deeper level, however, his defense of popular preaching and storytelling amounts to an argument for the continuing openness of the category of religious knowledge, for the possibility that humanity's understanding of the will of God was incomplete and susceptible to further refinement, even at the hands of individuals such as those preaching and telling stories to the Muslim masses.

On the one hand, ʿAlī b. Wafāʾ had to tread carefully. Zayn al-Dīn al-ʿIrāqī had insisted that the seers of visions should be individuals of recognized probity and character (*min ahl al-dīn waʾl-ʿadāla*), capable of distinguishing the true from the false. More pointedly, he observed that an individual who is asleep "is not legally responsible" (*laysa min ahl al-taklīf*) and so is not required to do anything he alleges he was ordered to do (i.e., by the Prophet) during his vision. Of course, he said, if that which the seer alleges is consistent with the Prophet's "settled law" (*sharīʿatahu ʾl-muqarrara*), then it is best that he perform the act allegedly required and leave off those forbidden by the vision. This judgment, however, relies upon the matter being settled in the law (*mashrūʿan*)—the vision merely confirms what the law had previously established. To al-ʿIrāqī's objections ʿAlī made a subtle response. He formally agreed with al-ʿIrāqī's final point, on the primacy of the law—al-ʿIrāqī's words were "correct" (*ṣaḥīḥ*), for "God did not take His prophet until he had completed for us our religion." But the thrust of his comments in fact left his reader in doubt about how "complete" the religion really was. The character of the individual relating his vision—that is, whether or not he is held to be legally responsible—speaks to the question of whether or not his audience should accept his account of his vision, he said, not whether the vision itself was valid. To be sure, if there were reason to doubt the trustworthiness of the seer of the vision, then it would not be incumbent upon anyone else to accept its message—just as, he said, if one whose witness is unreliable sees the new moon marking the start of Ramaḍān, he himself must begin his fast, but no one else need accept his testimony. But, once again, ʿAlī effectively left the question of the legitimacy of the vision reported to the audience to whom it was related; that is, he left considerable scope for storytellers and preachers to rely upon visions of the Prophet, and he left to their audiences the determination of their legitimacy and ethical force. And he pointedly reminded al-ʿIrāqī of Muḥammad's reported comment that "no mark of prophethood remains except the sound vision [*al-ruʾyā ʾl-ṣāliḥa*] seen by a Muslim."[64]

Like the reputable scholar that he was, al-ʿIrāqī returned to surer ground: that of the safe and secure transmission of knowledge. "Neither our teachers nor those who preceded them," he wrote, "ever alleged that knowledge had appeared to someone without [his] studying"—that is, without proper instruction (*mā raʾaynā wa-lā akhbaranā mashāyikhunā wa-lā man qablahum anna aḥad*[an] *ẓahara lahu ʿilm bi-ghayr taʿallum*). True knowledge, he seems to be saying, is that which is passed down from one's predecessors and secured by the authority of those who have gone before—which, of course, was not an uncommon attitude among medieval Muslim scholars. But ʿAlī was not convinced. "The absence of the sense of something [i.e., its immediate presence], let alone the absence of a report of it, does not indicate its non-existence," he reasoned (*ʿadam al-wijdān faḍl*[an] *ʿan ʿadam al-akhbār lā yadullu ʿalā ʿadam al-wujūd).* As proof, he cleverly offered the incontrovertible example of the Imām al-Shāfiʿī, who, he pointed out, had demonstrated matters concerning the science of jurisprudence which had never occurred to anyone previously. Anticipating the objection that al-Shāfiʿī had learned such matters because "he was inspired" (*ulhima*), ʿAlī replied that "inspiration is not acquired" (i.e., through efforts such as study [*al-ilhām lā yuktasabu*]). As for inspiration (*ilhām*) itself, said ʿAlī knowingly and approvingly, "how splendid is the path of the fair-minded!" (*mā aḥsan tarīqat al-munṣifīn*).[65] And, in doing so, ʿAlī found himself in good company: no less rigorous a critic than Ibn Taymiyya had defended the Sufi notion of individual inspiration (*ilḥām*) as, at least under certain limited circumstances, an acceptable source of juristic evidence.[66]

That would seem to leave the gates of knowledge open very wide indeed. Al-ʿIrāqī tried to fall back upon the foundations of faith, the Qurʾān and hadith, by citing a report common in the Sunni collections. The Prophet's cousin ʿAlī b. Abī Ṭālib was once asked whether the Prophet had ever granted him any special knowledge not entrusted to others. "No," he replied, "only the Qurʾān and what is in these pages, except that God has imparted to a servant an understanding of his book" (*lā inna al-qurʾān wa mā fī hadhihi ʾl-ṣaḥīfa illā an yuʾṭī allāh ʿabdan fahman fī kitābihi*). ʿAlī b. Wafāʾ thought that his interlocutor had just given up the game. "Allāhu akbar, Allāhu akbar!" he exclaimed. This hadith, in his opinion, was a "sufficient proof" (*ḥujja bāligha*) of his own point and "devastating to him who denies what one [or some] of the [spiritual] guides to truth and blessing set forth concerning private inspiration" (*kasran ʿalā man ankara mā jāʾa bihi baʿḍ al-murshidīn ilā ʾl-ḥaqq waʾl-khayr ʿan ilhām khuṣṣa bihi*).[67] ʿAlī's understanding of his famous namesake's words focused less on his denial of any special knowledge beyond Scripture than on his status as "a servant who understands." In other words, the issue was one of interpretation, and this, ʿAlī had already determined, was simply a matter of having a "sound heart." What, then, was there to prevent preachers and storytellers, too, from legitimately claiming private inspiration to interpret the scriptural foundations of the faith?

5 / Conclusion: Storytelling, Preaching, and the Problem of Religious Authority in Medieval Islam

ʿAlī b. Wafāʾ may or may not have been justified in thinking he had proved his point, that he had vindicated the popular preachers and storytellers and their role in the transmission of knowledge to the common people, but his confidence provides a convenient point at which to bring this discussion to a close. ʿAlī cannot categorically be said to have been correct—that is, to have had on his side the full weight of Muslim opinion—but neither could his interlocutor Zayn al-Dīn al-ʿIrāqī necessarily claim to represent a more "authentic" Islamic position, despite the long polemical tradition criticizing the activities and excesses of popular preachers and storytellers. What is interesting are both the terms of their debate, which I have tried to outline, and the very fact that at the turn of the eighth/fourteenth century the issues that divided them could remain so controversial. The problem festered, and not simply because the preachers and storytellers played an essential role in the transmission of religious knowledge to the Muslim masses, as Ibn al-Jawzī acknowledged, and so could not be dispensed with.

Lurking beneath the debate over popular preachers and storytellers is the larger and highly problematic question of religious authority in Islam. The absence of formal institutions of authority and the devolution of responsibility for interpreting the religion of the Prophet onto the shoulders of the scholars, as expressed through their consensus, is well known to Western historians. In itself, however, this observation cannot serve as a final statement on the issue. We must still seek to delineate more precisely the contours of and tensions embedded within Muslim conceptions of religious authority.

Something was different about the character of Islamic societies in the Near East during the Middle Period, those centuries that saw the crystallization of the debate over popular preaching, one that pitted scholars such as Ibn al-Jawzī against defenders of storytellers such as ʿAlī b. Wafāʾ. It was not a question of these societies having fallen away from a normative ideal associated with the "classical" period—indeed, that very terminology is deceiving. Such a viewpoint is in part a product of the familiar Islamic practice of projecting ideas and expressions backward onto earlier figures—Muḥammad himself, the respected caliph ʿUmar b. al-Khaṭṭāb, the Companions of the Prophet, and the early generations of Muslims generally—in order to lend them authority. Much recent research on a variety of topics has tended to undermine the assumption that characteristic features of Islam and of Islamic societies took shape at relatively early dates. Even so fundamental a principle as that of the authority of the ulama was, of course, a construct, one that emerged only after lengthy struggles with other possible loci of religious authority, including that of the caliph.[1] At least until the tenth and eleventh centuries many of the fundamental institutions and outlines of the Islamic tradition were highly contested.

But by the Middle Period, as a result of a variety of political and social factors—among them the eclipse of the centralized political authority of the ʿAbbāsid caliphs as well as increasing urbanization and the gradual transformation of Islam into a majority religion in most parts of the Near East—certain common social structures and patterns of social relationship began to mature. Chief among them was the emergence of the ulama as the principal arbiters of the Islamic tradition, as what Richard Bulliet called an "unappointed clergy."[2] The rise of the ulama was intimately connected to the emergence of the *sharīʿa* and its appurtenant forms and institutions as the dominant locus of Sunni Muslim self-definition. To say that Islam is a religion of the law, as the cliché would have it, is to point to a variety of conventions that were characteristic of medieval Islam: the institutions and personal networks through which Islamic learning was transmitted from one generation to the next; the coalescence of the four principal schools (*madhāhib*) of Sunni law, their mutual tolerance and the concomitant exclusion of others; and *fatwās*, answers to legal questions given by authorized scholars, which constituted for many Muslims their most direct experience of Islamic law.[3] All of these developments in different ways cast the ulama, and especially the specialists in law (*fuqahāʾ*), as the group best positioned to define what was and was not Islamic and made them the most effective wielders, not necessarily of power, but of religious authority.

The precise contours of their authority, however, as well as the definition of who qualified as one of the ulama, were never definitively delineated, and in the resulting ambiguity lay the seeds of continued controversy and struggle. The drama enacted itself on several different and overlapping levels. Since the ulama were usually so closely associated with the *sharīʿa,* with its definition and transmission, the legal front was inevitably one of the most hotly contested. In an oblique but important way the disagreement between opponents and defenders of the popular preachers and storytellers, particularly over the question of what constituted acceptable religious knowledge and the means of transmitting it, speaks to current debates about the medieval Muslim conception of the epistemological status of received religious knowledge, such as that involving the alleged "closing of the gates of independent reasoning" in Islamic jurisprudence. The traditional view, enunciated most clearly by the late Joseph Schacht, is that by the fourth/tenth century it was no longer possible for a scholar to exercise *ijtihād,* often translated as "independent reasoning" but which Schacht defined more precisely as "the drawing of valid conclusions from the Koran, the *sunna* of the Prophet, and the consensus, by analogy (*ḳiyās*) or systematic reasoning."[4] This view, according to which later Muslim jurists would be limited to the intellectual exercise of *taqlīd,* or "imitation" of the legal rules laid down by their predecessors, has recently come under sustained attack by historians who have argued that the use of *ijtihād* by Muslim jurists remained a theoretical possibility, and a practical necessity, at least through the end of the Middle Period.[5] The matter is complicated by the fact that *ijtihād,* in medieval juristic usage, could have radically different meanings, and, of course, the particular contours of a debate about the limits of jurisprudential thought are not directly germane to a discussion of preachers and storytellers. But several aspects of the debate strike me as relevant to the issue at hand.

In the first place, however *ijtihād* was defined, it is clear that some Muslim scholars recognized the possibility of substantial development and change in their understanding of the law—even if those who claimed the power of *ijtihād* sometimes engendered violent controversy[6]—and thus that Westerners who have seen medieval Islamic thought as ossified and stagnant have missed a vibrant epistemological debate at the heart of the intellectual traditions that went a good way toward defining medieval Islam. Second, as several very recent studies have demonstrated, that *ijtihād* continued in some form did not mean that the doctrine of *taqlīd* had no force or that there were no efforts to place significant restrictions on the scope of independent juristic thinking, whether those efforts were the product of government decrees or the more informal operation of the hierarchy of scholars themselves.[7] As Sherman Jackson has put it, *ijtihād* and *taqlīd* should not be seen as "mutually exclusive linear moments in Muslim history but rather [as] competing hegemonies that stood (and continue to stand) in perpetual competition with each other."[8] In other words, the controversy over *ijtihād* and *taqlīd* parallels the controversy over preachers and storytellers, both in that it points to a stratum of medieval Islamic religious thought which understood the character of religious knowledge to be open, flexible, and vibrant and also in that it suggests an effort on the part of the ulama to limit the range of permissible thought as well as the community of scholars privileged to participate in the process of shaping Islam.

Another aspect of the struggle, and one with more direct relevance to the question of popular preachers and storytellers, was that of Sufism. The story of the rapprochement of Sufism and the more formal Islam of the *fuqahā'* over the course of the Middle Period is well known. Al-Ghazālī (d. 505/1111) is frequently mentioned as a turning point in the process, but the story continued to develop for centuries after his death. As late as the seventh/thirteenth century in Egypt, the Shādhilī shaykh Ibn ʿAṭā' Allāh (d. 709/1309) absorbed from his grandfather a lingering suspicion of the mystical path but was converted by one of his teachers and ended up teaching both jurisprudence and *taṣawwuf* at the al-Azhar mosque.[9] The coming together of Sufism and the law can be traced on an institutional level, too, as *madrasas* devoted to instruction in jurisprudence came to house Sufi adepts and to support their worship, while *khānqāh*s established for the benefit of mystics began to offer lessons in *fiqh* and related sciences.[10] Even critics of certain aspects of Sufism (and of popular preaching), such as Ibn al-Jawzī and Ibn Taymiyya, were, famously, members of Sufi orders.[11]

But the tension between the mystical and jurisprudential modes of religious discourse was never thoroughly resolved, as the conflict over popular preachers would suggest. Whether or not Zayn al-Dīn al-ʿIrāqī cast his polemic against the storytellers explicitly as a critique of Sufis, it is not hard to detect in ʿAlī b. Wafā''s defense of them the influence of his own mystical orientation—as in, for example, his discussion of the concept of *ʿibra* and his apology for the acquisition of knowledge outside those channels through which the ulama sought to control it. A century and a half later the struggle raged on, sometimes in the same individual. ʿAbd al-

Wahhāb al-Shaʿrānī (d. 973/1565), for example, a prolific scholar of the Islamic sciences who respected the authority of the *sharīʿa,* nonetheless at one point sold all his books to take up study with an illiterate *shaykh.* He acknowledged the well-known Prophetic dictum that "the ulama are the heirs of the prophets" but thought that the tradition referred to transmitters of hadith (including, perhaps, storytellers?), rather than *fuqahāʾ,* who earned his scorn for their obsession with argumentation and intricate but unhelpful dialectic.[12] The point is not that Sufism and jurisprudential Islam did not in many ways grow closer during the Middle Period but, rather, that the tension between them was never thoroughly resolved and could occasionally break out in areas of sharp disagreement—as in the debate over popular preachers and storytellers.

It was not only in dialogue with jurisprudential Islam that Sufism encountered the problem of religious authority. At almost the same moment that ʿAlī b. Wafāʾ penned his treatise, the Sufis of Andalusia found themselves embroiled in a revealing dispute over the question of whether individuals could legitimately acquire knowledge and understanding of the mystical path through books only or whether a master had to supervise their training and education, a controversy studied some years ago by Muhsin Mahdi. Jurists who considered the question concluded naturally that those who risked studying Islamic mysticism without the supervision of an experienced *shaykh* flirted with disaster. But a more interesting response was that of the Sufi Ibn ʿAbbād al-Rundī (d. 792/1390), like ʿAlī b. Wafāʾ a member of the Shādhilī order and like him a popular preacher. Ibn ʿAbbād agreed that an adept should only study the texts of the mystical tradition under the aegis of a master but rejected the idea that all who sought mystical insight required the supervision of a *shaykh al-tarbiya* (master of training), as opposed to a *shaykh al-taʿlīm* (master of instruction). He pointed out that the great mystics of an earlier age, men such as al-Muḥāsibī and Abū Ṭālib al-Makkī, had disciplined themselves and trained their souls with only the informal and intermittent encouragement that they derived from contact with like-minded individuals. On the other hand, Ibn ʿAbbād acknowledged that, as Sufism had grown more popular, it had attracted as adepts those who perhaps lacked the firm moral character that undergirded the mystical discipline of al-Muḥāsibī, al-Makkī, and others; as a result, he observed, Sufis now placed great emphasis on identifying and submitting oneself to the supervision of a *shaykh al-tarbiya.* His analysis suggests a nostalgia for a time when those engaged in mystical pursuits were relatively few in number and limited to those of demonstrable inner strength. Behind it lay a remarkable transformation in the demographic foundations of Sufism. By the Middle Period in which Ibn ʿAbbād wrote, Sufism's popularity had brought ever larger numbers of Muslims to the path, not all of whom possessed what he felt were the requisite spiritual resources. His analysis stands in stark contrast to the more "democratic" vision of ʿAlī b. Wafāʾ, and in it we can perceive an effort on the part of Sufism itself to draw more tightly the lines of religious authority and to limit the range of those permitted to define the contours of the faith.[13]

All of this should be seen against the larger background of a progressive narrowing over the course of the Middle Period of the circle of knowledge recognized as acceptable by the ulama. Marshall Hodgson attributed this process principally to certain tendencies characteristic of societies committed to a monotheistic religion, such as the notion that human beings can discern that single truth that is or should be valid for all, tendencies compounded in medieval Islamic society by the fact that Near Eastern Muslims now came to constitute a decisive majority of the population.[14] Certain contingencies peculiar to the medieval period also must have played a critical role, in particular the sharp if not hermetic division between the ruling military elites, often Turkish in ethnicity and cultural orientation, and the native Muslim civilian populations, including, of course, the bulk of the ulama, over whom the soldiers ruled. The point is not that these regimes resulted in some sudden and novel bifurcation of political and religious authority but, rather, that their hegemony, coupled with the eclipse of the authority of the caliphs, encouraged the ulama to articulate more clearly and to defend more jealously a sphere of authority which was peculiarly their own. The Middle Period was a disruptive one, and devastating exogenous factors, such as the Crusader and Mongol invasions, as well as the calamitous assault of the plague in the fourteenth century, must have contributed to an atmosphere conducive to a "circling of the wagons."

Let me be clear: I am not arguing that Islamic society became over the course of the Middle Period intellectually or culturally stagnant, tied to a particular vision of the religion (i.e., of the truth) which was crystallized for all time and one that inhibited intellectual speculation and growth. On the contrary, the societies of the medieval Islamic Near East, as well as their cultural traditions, remained vibrant and dynamic. Even in areas such as the natural sciences, which Western scholars have often assumed to have suffered from decay and stagnation in the Middle Period, the Islamic world continued to see much development and growth.[15] Moreover, of course, no society can completely immunize itself from historical change, and even those that purport to represent timeless and permanent social and cultural arrangements are themselves subject to evolution, even if that evolution is obscured by the ideology of permanence.[16] But I do think that many of the medieval ulama would have preferred a more static vision and experience of their faith tradition and that their vision be shared by others. Their preference is visible in the law, especially in the growing role in legal education of compendia of legal rules (*mukhtaṣars*) which sought both to restrict the numbers of those scholars to whom (relatively) unfettered reasoning was permitted and also to encourage "univocality" within each *madhhab*.[17] It is visible, too, more broadly in the discourse over innovations which characterized one strand of medieval Islamic polemic, one closely related to that hostile to popular preachers and storytellers. The normative distinction between that which was *sunna,* meaning accepted practice associated with the Prophet and his companions, and that which was *bidʿa,* illegitimate innovation, was an old one in Islamic discourse, but some traditionalist scholars addressed it with particular ferocity in the Middle Period and sought to use it to construct defenses against certain religious practices of which they disapproved—including that of popular preaching and storytelling.[18]

Were the scholars successful in permanently narrowing the scope of the "truth" and the circle of those permitted to define it? An answer to such a question lies well beyond the topical and chronological scope of this book, and indeed the question itself may be ahistorical. But what is clear, I think, is that the ulama's struggle in the Middle Period against innovations and practices such as popular preaching was part of a process through which they sought to exert control over a religious tradition that, lacking formal institutions and mechanisms of authority, was inherently vibrant and polymorphous. At the same time, it is important to stress the fact that the process was contested, that scholars such as Ibn al-Jawzī, Zayn al-Dīn al-ʿIrāqī, and Jalāl al-Dīn al-Suyūṭī did not speak for all Muslims in their articulation of a viewpoint of what constituted Islam. Alternatively, we might wish to reverse the order of emphasis. In reaction to outdated Western views of a static, unchanging Islam, historians and anthropologists have in recent decades stressed the openness and flexibility of Islamic societies and their constructions of Islam.[19] The debate over popular preachers and storytellers reminds us that, nonetheless, religious authority was a very real and compelling (if unresolvable) issue and that some influential Muslims would have defined that authority and its social base much more precisely and narrowly.

In short, the debate over popular preachers and storytellers was characteristic of broader trends and tensions visible at the intersection of the Islamic religion and the societies of medieval Muslims. On the critical question of religious authority Muslims continued to the end of the Middle Period to construct demonstrably different and competing answers. On the one hand, it is worth noting that ʿAlī b. Wafāʾ's voice in praise of popular preachers and storytellers seems to have been a relatively lonely one. I am not aware of any other treatises composed during the Islamic Middle Period which were devoted specifically to defending the *quṣṣāṣ* and *wuʿʿāẓ* against their critics; even this treatise apparently survives in a unique manuscript, which must raise questions about how widely it circulated. Zayn al-Dīn al-ʿIrāqī, by contrast, could draw upon an extensive polemical tradition that outlined the case against the storytellers; his concerns were shared by scholars as diverse in time and domicile as Ibn al-Jawzī, Ibn Taymiyya, and al-Suyūṭī. On the other hand, we may be right in suspecting that ʿAlī b. Wafāʾ spoke for a chorus of voices lost to posterity. Their fiercest critics, such as Ibn al-Jawzī, acknowledged the important role that preachers and storytellers played in transmitting religious lore and instruction to the Muslim masses. Sufi orders such as the Shādhiliyya, and especially its Wafāʾī branch, acquired a reputation for preaching, so much so that individual preachers of a scholarly background could be said to have spoken "in the manner of the Banūʾl-Wafāʾ."

In any case it clearly emerges from the historical record that popular preaching and storytelling raised profound and troubling issues of authority—social, political, and intellectual—for medieval Muslim societies. The anecdotes of fake and fraudulent preachers bandied about by al-Jawbarī, Ibn al-Jawzī, and others represent only the most colorful aspects of a much larger problem. If, as ʿAlī b. Wafāʾ seems to suggest, some preachers and storytellers were in a position to supplement the consensus of the scholars about what constituted permissible religious thought and behavior, then their activities placed them at the heart of the ongoing process of redefining Islam, at least as far as their audiences were concerned. And, of course, their audiences constituted a good portion of those who identified themselves as Muslim.

Consequently, we can appreciate the concern of individuals such as al-Suyūṭī that popular preachers and storytellers threatened the fragile edifice of religious knowledge which had been so laboriously constructed over the centuries. From the standpoint of both traditionalists such as Ibn Taymiyya and also those modern scholars who may have defined *Islam* in categorical terms, the attitude and activities of preachers and storytellers appear troubling, to say the least. Islam, like any other religious tradition, is culturally constructed and contingent upon the circumstances and viewpoints of those who claim it as their own. In the end the category of religious knowledge, and thus the very definition of Islam as it was understood by the common people who attended the circles led by ʿAlī b. Wafāʾ and others like him, remained throughout the Middle Period porous and flexible but, above all, contested, thanks in part to the activities of popular preachers and storytellers.

Notes

INTRODUCTION

1. The *locus classicus* of this critique, of course, is Edward Said, *Orientalism* (New York: Vintage, 1978). For a spirited defense of the tradition of academic Orientalism, see Bernard Lewis, "The Question of Orientalism," *New York Review of Books,* 24 June 1982, 49–56.

2. See Clifford Geertz, "Thick Description: Toward an Interpretive Theory of Culture," *The Interpretation of Culture* (New York: Basic Books, 1973), 3–30.

3. Clifford Geertz, *Islam Observed: Religious Development in Morocco and Indonesia* (New Haven: Yale University Press, 1968), 4.

4. Cf., for example, Muhammad Umar Memon, *Ibn Taimiya's Struggle against Popular Religion* (The Hague: Mouton, 1976); and Boaz Shoshan, *Popular Culture in Medieval Cairo* (Cambridge: Cambridge University Press, 1993).

5. Christopher S. Taylor, *In the Vicinity of the Righteous: Ziyāra and the Veneration of Muslim Saints in Late Medieval Egypt* (Leiden: E. J. Brill, 1998); Jonathan Berkey, *The Transmission of Knowledge in Medieval Cairo: A Social History of Islamic Education* (Princeton: Princeton University Press, 1992), esp. 182–218; Ahmet Karamustafa, *God's Unruly Friends: Dervish Groups in the Islamic Later Middle Period, 1200–1500* (Salt Lake City: University of Utah Press 1994).

6. Theodor Nöldeke, *Sketches from Eastern History,* trans. John Sutherland Black (1892; rpt., Beirut: Khayats, 1963), 15–19.

7. The injunction can be found in slightly different forms throughout the Qur'ān, for example, at 3:104, 110, 114; 9:112; 22:41; 31:17.

8. al-Bukhārī, *Ṣaḥīḥ,* "Kitāb al-Jumʿa," *Bāb* 2, no. 877, and 13, no. 888; Aḥmad b. Ḥajar al-ʿAsqalānī, *Fatḥ al-bārī bi-sharḥ ṣaḥīḥ al-bukhārī,* ed. ʿAbd al-ʿAzīz b. Bāz, 16 vols. (Beirut: Dār al-Fikr, 1995), 3:7, 30.

9. On the subject of the connection between various literary genres in the

early Islamic period, see A. A. Duri, *The Rise of Historical Writing among the Arabs,* trans. Lawrence Conrad (Princeton: Princeton University Press, 1983).

10. Mia I. Gerhardt, *The Art of Storytelling: A Literary Study of the Thousand and One Nights* (Leiden: E. J. Brill, 1963), 341.

11. Lawrence Stone, "The Revival of Narrative: Reflections on a New Old History," *Past and Present* 85 (1979): 3–24; Natalie Zemon Davis, *Fiction in the Archives: Pardon Tales and Their Tellers in Sixteenth-Century France* (Stanford: Stanford University Press, 1987).

12. ʿAbd al-Raḥmān b. ʿAlī b. al-Jawzī, *Kitāb al-quṣṣāṣ waʾl-mudhakkirīn,* ed. Merlin Swartz (Beirut: Dar al-Machreq, 1986), 13–14 (Eng. trans., 99–100). The best-known example is probably that of Muhammad's speech during the "farewell pilgrimage" toward the end of his life; see Ibn Isḥaq, *Sīrat rasūl allāh,* trans. Alfred Guillaume, *The Life of Muhammad* (Oxford: Oxford University Press, 1955), 651.

13. *EI,* 2d ed., art. "MINBAR" (by J. Pedersen). On the origin of the *miḥrāb,* see Oleg Grabar, *Formation of Islamic Art* (New Haven: Yale University Press, 1973), 120–22.

14. See, for example, Michael Gilsenan, *Recognizing Islam: Religion and Society in the Modern Middle East* (London: I. B. Tauris, 1992), esp. 19.

15. See Burke's conclusion to the edited volume of Hodgson's essays, *Rethinking World History: Essays on Europe, Islam, and World History,* ed. Edmund Burke III (Cambridge: Cambridge University Press, 1993), 301–28, esp. 314–19.

16. Patrick Gaffney, *The Prophet's Pulpit: Islamic Preaching in Contemporary Egypt* (Berkeley: University of California Press, 1994), 27.

17. Geertz, *Islam Observed,* 55.

18. Gaffney, *Prophet's Pulpit,* 30.

19. Gilsenan, *Recognizing Islam,* 19.

20. Marshall G. S. Hodgson, *The Venture of Islam: Conscience and History in a World Civilization,* 3 vols. (Chicago: University of Chicago Press, 1974), 2:3–11. I accept the arguments of Hodgson and others that the phrase *Middle Ages,* drawn from the historiography of Europe, is potentially misleading in the Islamic context. The commonly accepted alternative, however—Hodgson's *Islamic Middle Period*—does not easily render itself into an adjectival form. Accordingly, I have retained use of the adjective *medieval.*

21. See, for example, the review essay of Natalie Zemon Davis, "From 'Popular Religion' to Religious Culture," in *Reformation Europe: A Guide to Research,* ed. Steven Ozment (St. Louis: Center for Reformation Research, 1982), 321–41.

22. Shoshan, *Popular Culture in Medieval Cairo,* 7.

23. Ibid. It is such "texts," ranging from a popular biography of the Prophet

to the Egyptian festival of Nawrūz, which form the subject of Shoshan's interesting book.

24. A model study of this phenomenon is Taylor's investigation of the visitation of tombs in the medieval Cairene cemeteries, *In the Vicinity of the Righteous.*

25. Karamustafa, *God's Unruly Friends,* esp. 4–11.

26. Ibid., 5.

27. On the problem of identifying an "orthodoxy" in the Islamic tradition, see Bernard Lewis, "The Significance of Heresy in Islam," *Studia Islamica* 1 (1953): 43–63; and Alexander Knysh, "'Orthodoxy' and 'Heresy' in Medieval Islam: An Essay in Reassessment," *Muslim World* 83 (1993): 48–67.

28. Davis, "From 'Popular Religion' to Religious Culture," 323–24.

29. Emmanuel Leroy Ladurie, *Montaillou: Promised Land of Error* (New York: George Braziller, 1978).

30. Davis, "From 'Popular Religion' to Religious Culture," 323.

31. *EI,* 2d ed., art. "KHUṬBA" (by A. J. Wensinck); G. E. Von Grunebaum, *Muhammadan Festivals* (1951; rpt., New York: Olive Branch Press, 1988), 11.

32. Aḥmad b. ʿAlī al-Qalqashandī, *Ṣubḥ al-aʿshā fī ṣinaʿat al-inshā',* 14 vols. (Cairo: al-Mu'assasa al-Miṣriyya al-ʿĀmma li'l-Ta'līf wa'l-Tarjama wa'l-Ṭibāʿa wa'l-Nashr, 1964), 4:39.

33. Muslim, *Ṣaḥīḥ,* "Jumʿa," no. 47; A. J. Wensinck, *Concordances et indices de la tradition musulmane* (Leiden: E. J. Brill, 1943), 2:48.

34. al-Qalqashandī, *Ṣubḥ al-aʿshā,* 5:463.

35. Ibn Khaldūn, *The Muqaddimah,* trans. Franz Rosenthal, 3 vols., 2d ed. (Princeton: Princeton University Press, 1980), 2:70–73.

36. Paula Sanders, *Ritual, Politics, and the City in Fatimid Cairo* (Albany: SUNY Press, 1994), 44.

37. Richard W. Bulliet, *The Patricians of Nishapur: A Study in Medieval Islamic Social History* (Cambridge, Mass.: Harvard University Press, 1972), 66.

38. Tāj al-Dīn ʿAbd al-Wahhāb al-Subkī, *Muʿīd al-niʿam wa mubīd al-niqam,* ed. David W. Myhrman (London: Luzac, 1908), 160–63; see also George Makdisi, *The Rise of Colleges: Institutions of Learning in Islam and the West* (Edinburgh: Edinburgh University Press, 1981), 217–18; Berkey, *Transmission of Knowledge in Medieval Cairo,* 204–6.

39. ʿAbd al-Raḥīm b. Muḥammad b. Nubāta al-Fāriqī, *Dīwān khuṭab* (Beirut: Maṭbaʿat Jarīdat Bayrūt, 1311 A.H.).

40. Ibn al-Jawzī, *Kitāb al-quṣṣāṣ wa'l-mudhakkirīn,* 11 (Eng. trans., 97–98).

41. Edward William Lane, *An Account of the Manners and Customs of the Modern Egyptians,* 5th ed. (1860; rpt., New York: Dover, 1973), 391–413.

42. Cited by Ignaz Goldziher, *Muslim Studies,* 2 vols., trans. C. R. Barber and S. M. Stern (London: George Allen and Unwin, 1966), 2:145–63.

43. Peter Heath, *The Thirsty Sword: Sīrat ʿAntar and the Arabic Popular Epic* (Salt Lake City: University of Utah Press, 1996), 29, 170–72. See also David Pinault's analysis of the tale of "The City of Brass" from the *Thousand and One Nights,* in *Story-telling Techniques in the Arabian Nights* (Leiden: E. J. Brill, 1992), 231–37.

44. Among the more important recent studies: Bulliet, *The Patricians of Nishapur;* Makdisi, *The Rise of Colleges;* and, most recently, Michael Chamberlain, *Knowledge and Social Practice in Damascus, 1190–1350* (Cambridge: Cambridge University Press, 1994).

45. Berkey, *Transmission of Knowledge,* 182–218.

46. Specifically mentioned by al-Subkī, *Muʿīd al-niʿam,* 162–63.

47. On this, see Jonathan P. Berkey, "Tradition, Innovation, and the Social Construction of Knowledge in the Medieval Islamic Near East," *Past and Present* 146 (1995): 38–65.

48. Quite a few collections of Ibn al-Jawzī's sermons survive, and several have been published. See, for example, *Kitāb al-lutf fi'l-waʿẓ* (Beirut: Dār al-Kutub al-ʿIlmiyya, 1984); and *al-Yāqūta fi'l-waʿẓ* (Cairo: ʿĪsā al-Bābī al-Ḥalabī, 1351 A.H.).

49. Ibn Nubāta, *Dīwān khuṭab,* esp. 275f; *EI,* 2d ed., art. "IBN NUBĀTA" (by M. Canard).

50. The standard work on the genre of the legends of the prophets is that of Tilman Nagel, *Die Qiṣaṣ al-Anbiyā'. Ein Beitrag zur arabischen Literaturgeschichte* (Bonn: Rheinische Friedrich-Wilhems-Universität, 1967); *EI,* 2d ed., art. "ḲIṢAṢ AL-ANBIYĀ'" (by T. Nagel).

51. Ed. Muḥammad al-Ṣabbāgh (Beirut: al-Maktab al-Islāmī, 1972).

52. On Shaykh Shuʿayb, see Ibn Ḥajar al-ʿAsqalānī, *Inbā' al-ghumr bi-abnā' al-ʿumr,* 9 vols. (Haydarabad: Dā'irat al-Maʿārif al-ʿUthmāniyya, 1975), 4:63–64; Muḥammad ibn ʿAbd al-Raḥmān al-Sakhāwī, *al-Ḍaw' al-lāmiʿ li-ahl al-qarn al-tāsiʿ,* 12 vols. (Cairo: Maktabat al-Quds, 1934), 5:20. On the Ḥarāfīsh, see William Brinner, "The Significance of the *Ḥarāfīsh* and Their 'Sultan,'" *JESHO* 6 (1963): 190–215; on the uncertainty surrounding al-Ḥurayfīsh's name and identity, see ibid., 210n.

53. al-Ḥurayfīsh, *al-Rawḍ al-fā'iq fi'l-mawāʿiẓ wa'l-raqā'iq* (Cairo: Muṣṭafā 'l-Bābī al-Ḥalabī, 1949).

54. The text refers occasionally to the "people of this circle" (*ahl hādhihi 'l-majālis*), for example, at fol. 55r.

55. Johannes Pedersen, "The Criticism of the Islamic Preacher," *Die Welt des Islams,* n.s., 2 (1953): 230.

56. For a thought-provoking critique of the very notion of education as a discrete process in a medieval Islamic society, see Chamberlain, *Knowledge and Social Practice in Damascus,* and my review of the book in *American Historical Review* 101 (1996): 1254–56.

57. *Sūra* 49, vv. 11, 13. See also Fazlur Rahman, *Major Themes of the Quran* (Minneapolis: Bibliotheca Islamica, 1980), 45.

58. *Sūra* 33, v. 35; Rahman, *Major Themes,* 49–50. On Qur'ānic egalitarianism, see Louise Marlow, *Hierarchy and Egalitarianism in Islamic Thought* (Cambridge: Cambridge University Press, 1997), 2–4.

1 / ORIGINS AND EARLY CONTROVERSY

1. Much of the earlier secondary material dwelt upon this issue; see now Khalil 'Athamina, "Al-Qasas: Its Emergence, Religious Origin and Its Socio-political Impact on Early Muslim Society," *Studia Islamica* 76 (1992): 53–74.

2. Jalāl al-Dīn al-Suyūṭī, *Taḥdhīr al-khawāṣṣ min akādhīb al-quṣṣāṣ,* ed. Muḥammad al-Sabbāgh (Beirut: al-Maktab al-Islāmī, 1972), 171–72. Ibn al-Jawzī, in his book *Kitāb al-quṣṣāṣ wa'l-mudhakkirīn,* ed. Merlin L. Swartz (Beirut: Dar el-Machreq, 1971), 22 (Eng. trans., 108), gives a slightly different version of the report, identifying Tamīm as the first *qāṣṣ.*

3. *EI,* 1st ed., art. "TAMĪM AL-DĀRĪ" (by G. Levi della Vida).

4. Abū Bakr Muḥammad al-Ṭurṭūshī, *Kitāb al-ḥawādith wa 'l-bidaʿ,* ed. A. M. Turki (Beirut: Dār al-Gharb al-Islāmī, 1990), 228; Ibn al-Jawzī, *Kitāb al-quṣṣāṣ wa'l-mudhakkirīn,* 127–28 (Eng. trans., 211–12).

5. 'Athamina, "Al-Qasas," 53–65.

6. Ibid., 63. Cf. the remark of Ibn al-Jawzī, who insisted that "in older times, preachers [*wuʿʿāẓ*] were scholars and jurists [*ʿulamā' fuqahā'*]." *Talbīs iblīs* (Beirut: Dūr al-Kutub al-ʿIlmiyya, n.d.), 123.

7. Gordon Newby, "Tafsir Isra'iliyat: The Development of Qur'an Commentary in Early Islam in Its Relationship to Judaeo-Christian Traditions of Scriptural Commentary," in *Studies in Qur'an and Tafsir,* ed. Alford T. Welch, *Journal of the American Academy of Religion* 47, Thematic issue 4S (1980): 689.

8. See, for example, al-Ṭurṭūshī, *Kitāb al-ḥawādith wa'l-bidaʿ,* 233–34; 'Athamina, "Al-Qasas," 65–74.

9. al-Suyūṭī, *Taḥdhīr al-khawāṣṣ,* 172; see also Ibn al-Jawzī, *Kitāb al-quṣṣāṣ wa'l-mudhakkirīn,* 28–29 (Eng. trans., 114–15). Other versions of the hadith replace *murā'ī* with *mukhtāl* (deceitful) or *mutakallaf* (false).

10. Charles Pellat, *Le Milieu basrien et la formation de Ǧāḥiẓ* (Paris: Librairie

d'Amérique et d'Orient, 1953), 108–16. Al-Jāḥiẓ provides a list of some of the *quṣṣāṣ* of Baṣra in *al-Bayān wa'l-tabyīn,* ed. ʿAbd al-Salām Muḥammad Hīrān, 4 vols. (Cairo: al-Khāngī, 1975), 306–8.

11. G. H. A. Juynboll, *Muslim Tradition: Studies in Chronology, Provenance, and Authorship of Early Ḥadīth* (Cambridge: Cambridge University Press, 1983), 12.

12. Ibn al-Jawzī, *Kitāb al-quṣṣāṣ wa'l-mudhakkirīn,* 20–21 (Eng. trans., 107).

13. Ibid., 230 (Eng. trans., 144).

14. Ibid., 108 (Eng. trans., 192); see also Ignaz Goldziher, *Muslim Studies,* trans. C. R. Barber and S. M. Stern, 2 vols. (London: George Allen and Unwin, 1966), 2:157.

15. Ibn al-Jawzī, *Kitāb al-quṣṣāṣ wa'l-mudhakkirīn,* 97–98 (Eng. trans., 177–78); Goldziher, *Muslim Studies,* 2:157–58.

16. Ed. Muḥammad al-Ṣabbāgh (Beirut: al-Maktab al-Islāmī, 1972).

17. al-Suyūṭī, *Taḥdhīr al-khawāṣṣ,* 4. Cf. a similar story told by Abū Bakr Aḥmad b. ʿAlī al-Khaṭīb al-Baghdādī, *Tārīkh baghdād,* 14 vols. (Beirut: Dār al-Kitāb al-ʿArabī, 1966), 2:386–90.

18. al-Suyūṭī, *Taḥdhīr al-khawāṣṣ,* 136.

19. al-Khaṭīb al-Baghdādī, *Tārīkh baghdād,* 1:359–60.

20. ʿAbd al-Raḥmān b. ʿAlī b. al-Jawzī, *al-Muntaẓam fī tārīkh al-mulūk wa'l-umam,* 10 vols. (Haydarabad: Dā'irat al-Maʿārif al-ʿUthmāniyya, 1359 A.H.), 9:75–76, 140.

21. Tāj al-Dīn ʿAbd al-Wahhāb al-Shaʿrānī, *al-Ṭabaqāt al-ṣughrā,* ed. ʿAbd al-Qādir Ahmad ʿAtā (Cairo: Maktabat al-Qāhira, 1970), 77. Cf. al-Shaʿrānī's story about Shams al-Dīn Muḥammad al-Dīrūṭī (d. 921/1515), *al-Ṭabaqāṭ al-kubrā,* 2 vols. (Cairo: Muḥammad ʿAlī Ṣubayḥ, 1965), 2:164–65.

22. Aḥmad b. Ḥajar al-ʿAsqalānī, *al-Durar al-kāmina fī aʿyān al-mi'a al-thāmina,* ed. Muḥammad Sayyid Jād al-Ḥaqq, 5 vols. (Cairo: Dār al-Kutub al-Ḥadītha, 1966), 1:291–93.

23. *Qubayr jā'aka dubayr.* Muḥammad b. ʿAbd al-Raḥīm b. al-Furāt, *Tārīkh,* ed. Qusṭanṭīn Zurayq and Najlā ʿIzz al-Dīn, vols. 7–9 (Beirut: American University in Beirut Press, 1936–42), 8:72–73; Khalīl b. Aybak al-Ṣafadī, *al-Wāfī bi'l-wafiyyāt,* 2d ed. (Wiesbaden: Frank Steiner Verlag, 1962–), 6:147–48; Abū'l-Maḥāsin Yūsuf b. Taghrī Birdī, *al-Manhal al-ṣāfī wa'l-mustawfī baʿd al-wāfī,* ed. Muḥammad M. Amīn, 7 vols. to date (Cairo: al-Hay'a al-Miṣriyya al-ʿĀmma li'l-Kitāb, 1984–), 1:177–78.

24. ʿAlī b. Dā'ūd b. al-Ṣayrafi al-Jawharī, *Nuzhat al-nufūs wa'l-abdān fī tawārīkh al-zamān,* ed. Ḥasan Ḥabashī (Cairo: Wizārat al-Thaqāfa, 1970), 1:419; Aḥmad b. Ḥajar al-ʿAsqalānī, *al-Durar al-kāmina,* 4:114–15; idem, *Inbā' al-ghumr bi-abnā'*

al-ʿumr, 9 vols. (Haydarabad: Dāʾirat al-Maʿārif al-ʿUthmāniyya, 1967–76), 3:271–72; Abū'l-Maḥāsin Yūsuf b. Taghrī Birdī, *al-Nujūm al-zāhira fī mulūk miṣr wa'l-qāhira,* 16 vols. (Cairo: al-Hay'a al-Miṣriyya al-ʿĀmma li'l-Ta'līf wa'l-Nashr, 1929–72), 12:146–48; ʿAbd al-Ḥayy b. Aḥmad b. al-ʿImād, *Shadharāt al-dhahab fī akhbār man dhahab,* 8 vols. (Cairo: Maktabat al-Qudsī, 1931–32), 6:351.

25. Aḥmad b. ʿAlī al-Maqrīzī, *al-Sulūk li-maʿrifat duwal al-mulūk,* 4 vols. in 12, ed. Muḥammad Muṣṭafā Ziyāda and Saʿīd ʿAbd al-Fattāḥ ʿĀshūr (Cairo: Lajnat al-Ta'līf wa'l-Tarjama wa'l-Nashr, 1956–73), 3:685–86; Ibn Taghrī Birdī, *al-Nujūm al-zāhira,* 11:385; Ibn al-Ṣayrafī, *Nuzhat al-nufūs,* 1:277. Cf. Ibn al-Furāt, *Tārīkh,* 9:173–74, who explicitly identifies his earlier occupation as having "made and sold the ink with which one writes."

26. Johannes Pedersen, "The Criticism of the Islamic Preacher," *Die Welt des Islams,* n.s., 2 (1953): 215–31; Merlin L. Swartz, *Ibn al-Jawzī's Kitāb al-Quṣṣāṣ wa'l-Mudhakkirīn* (Beirut: Dar el-Machreq, 1971), 55–60. The most important published treatises criticizing the *quṣṣāṣ* are those of Ibn al-Jawzī, published by Swartz, and of Jalāl al-Din al-Suyūṭī, *Taḥdhīr al-khawāṣṣ,* cited earlier. Al-Suyūṭī's treatise contains lengthy excerpts from a lost work of Zayn al-Dīn al-ʿIrāqī (d. 806/1404), to which *al-Bāʿith ʿalā 'l-khalāṣ* is a point-by-point response. (See n. 56.) Criticism of various practices of the storytellers can also be found in other works, such al-Ghazālī's famous *Iḥyā' ʿulūm al-dīn,* and *Madkhal al-sharʿ al-sharīf,* by Ibn al-Ḥājj al-ʿAbdarī (d. 737/1336).

27. See his remarks in *Kitāb al-mawḍūʿāt,* 2d ed., 3 vols., ed. ʿAbd al-Raḥmān Muḥammad ʿUthmān (Cairo: Dār al-Fikr, 1983), 1:45.

28. Swartz, *Ibn al-Jawzī's Kitāb al-Quṣṣāṣ,* 26–36.

29. Idrīs b. Baydakīn al-Turkumānī, *Kitāb al-lumaʿ fī 'l-ḥawādith wa 'l-bidaʿ,* ed. Ṣubḥī Labīb (Wiesbaden: Franz Steiner Verlag, 1986), 178–79.

30. Pedersen, "Criticism of the Islamic Preacher," 222; Abū Ṭālib al-Makkī, *Qūt al-qulūb fī muʿāmalat al-maḥbūb wa-waṣf ṭarīq al-murīd ilā maqām al-tawḥīd,* ed. Bāsil ʿUyūn al-Sūd, in 2 vols. (Beirut: Dār al-Kutub al-ʿIlmiyya, 1997), 1:267–73. Al-Makkī's opinion was repeated by later critics, including the stern Mālikī jurist Ibn al-Ḥājj, in *Madkhal al-sharʿ al-sharīf,* 2:146. See also al-Suyūṭī, *Taḥdhīr al-khawāṣṣ,* 215–16. Al-Makkī, however, as a transmitter of hadith, also objected to the storytellers' recitation of false traditions (Swartz, *Ibn al-Jawzī's Kitāb al-Quṣṣāṣ,* 57).

31. See Ignaz Goldziher, *Muslim Studies,* trans. C. R. Barber and S. M. Stern (London: George Allen and Unwin, 1966), 2:1445–63. If Patricia Crone is right, there is a delicious historical irony here, for she has argued that the storytellers were responsible for the fabrication and the corruption of the bulk of the material that constitutes the accepted Islamic tradition itself, and in particular the gen-

erally accepted accounts of the origin and rise of Islam. See *Meccan Trade and the Rise of Islam* (Oxford: Basil Blackwell, 1987), 203–30.

32. Ibn al-Jawzī, *Kitāb al-mawḍūʿāt,* 1:29, 32.

33. Ibn al-Ḥājj, *Madkhal al-sharʿ al-sharīf,* 2:14.

34. al-Suyūṭī, *Taḥdhīr al-khawāṣṣ,* 71–73; see also M. J. Kister, "Ḥaddithū ʿan banī isrā'īl wa-lā ḥaraja: A Study of an Early Tradition," *Israel Oriental Studies* 2 (1972): 215–39, esp. 217–20.

35. al-Suyūṭī, *Taḥdhīr al-khawāṣṣ,* 67 f.

36. Ibid., 162. Other estimates, dutifully recorded by al-Suyūṭī, also circulated. Cf. Ibn al-Jawzī, *Kitāb al-mawḍūʿāt,* 1:38, in which he gives the figure of fourteen thousand.

37. Cited in Ibn al-Ḥājj, *Madkhal al-sharʿ al-sharīf,* 2:146; and AbuṬālib al-Makkī, *Qūt al-qulūb,* 1:272.

38. al-Turtūshī, *Kitāb al-ḥawādith wa'l-bidaʿ,* 231–32. The story can also be found in Abu Ṭālib al-Makkī, *Qūt al-qulūb,* 1:272.

39. C. E. Bosworth, *The Medieval Islamic Underground: The Banū Sāsān in Arabic Society and Literature,* 2 vols. (Leiden: E. J. Brill, 1976), 1:88, 111–12.

40. ʿAbd al-Raḥīm b. ʿUmar al-Jawbarī, *al-Mukhtār min kashf al-asrār* (Damascus, 1302 A.H.), 33–38; *Le Voile arraché,* trans. René Khawam (Paris: Phebus, 1979), 91–101. See also Bosworth, *Medieval Islamic Underground,* 291; and Ibn al-Jawzī, *Kitāb al-quṣṣāṣ wa'l-mudhakkirīn,* 93–94 (Eng. trans., 171).

41. Ibn al-Jawzī, *Kitāb al-quṣṣāṣ wa'l-mudhakkirīn,* 121 (Eng. trans., 206); al-Suyūṭī, *Taḥdhīr al-khawāṣṣ,* 136.

42. Ibn al-Jawzī, *Kitāb al-quṣṣāṣ wa'l-mudhakkirīn,* 125–26 (Eng. trans., 210); ʿAlī b. Maymūn al-Idrīsī, *Bayān ghurbat al-islām bi-wāsiṭat ṣinfay al-mutafaqqiha wa'l-mutafaqqira min ahl miṣr wa'l-shām wa mā yalīhima min bilād al-aʿjām,* Princeton Garret Ms. 828H, fol. 68v–69r.

43. Ibn al-Ḥājj, *Madkhal al-sharʿ al-sharīf,* 2:271.

44. Ibn al-Jawzī, *Kitāb al-quṣṣāṣ wa'l-mudhakkirīn,* 118 (Eng. trans., 203); Zayn al-Dīn al-ʿIrāqī, as quoted in *al-Bāʿith ʿalā 'l-khalāṣ,* fol. 2v. On the innovation of chanting the Qur'ān, see al-Ṭurṭūshī, *Ḥawādith,* 183–93; and Maribel Fierro, "The Treatises against Innovations (*kutub al-bidʿa*)," *Der Islam* 69 (1992): 211–13.

45. al-Suyūṭī, *Taḥdhīr al-khawāṣṣ,* 3; Ibn al-Hājj, *Madkhal al-sharʿ al-sharīf,* 2:144–67 f.

46. Vardit Rispler, "Toward a New Understanding of the Term *Bidʿa,*" *Der Islam* 68 (1991): 320–28.

47. al-Suyūṭī, *Taḥdhīr al-khawāṣṣ,* 189; Zayn al-Dīn al-ʿIrāqī, quoted in B.L. Or. 4275, fol. 11r.

48. Ibn al-Jawzī, *Kitāb al-quṣṣāṣ wa'l-mudhakkirīn,* 37, 127 (Eng. trans., 122–23, 211).

49. al-Idrīsī, *Bayān ghurbat al-islām,* fol. 64v.

50. Ibid., fol. 60v.

51. Ibn al-Jawzī, *Kitāb al-quṣṣāṣ wa'l-mudhakkirīn,* 142 (Eng. trans., 226).

52. Ibn al-Ḥājj, *Madkhal al-sharʿ al-sharīf,* 1:268 and 2:16 (on the *hatk al-ḥarīm*). On Ibn al-Ḥājj's attitudes toward women and their participation in public aspects of urban culture, see Huda Lutfi, "Manners and Customs of Fourteenth-Century Cairene Women: Female Anarchy versus Male Sharʿi Order in Muslim Prescriptive Treatises," in *Women in Middle Eastern History: Shifting Boundaries in Sex and Gender,* ed. Nikki Keddie and Beth Baron (New Haven: Yale University Press, 1991), 99–121.

53. Ibn al-Jawzī, *Kitāb al-quṣṣāṣ wa'l-mudhakkirīn,* 117 (Eng. trans., 203). See also a similar passage in Ibn al-Ḥājj, *Madkhal al-sharʿ al-sharīf,* 2:16.

54. See, for example, al-Baghdādī, *Tārīkh Baghdād,* 14:446–47; and Ibn al-Jawzī, *al-Muntaẓam,* 8:128, 10:7–8; Abū'l-Muẓaffar Yūsuf Sibṭ b. al-Jawzī, *Mir'āt al-zamān fī tārīkh al-aʿyān,* vol. 8 in 2 (Haydarabad: Dā'irat al-Maʿārif al-ʿUthmāniyya. 1951–52), 1:126–27.

55. Ibn al-Ḥājj, *Madkhal al-sharʿ al-sharīf,* 2:12–14.

56. B.L. Or. 4275; see Charles Rieu, *Supplement to the Catalogue of the Arabic Manuscripts in the British Museum* (London: Longmans, 1894), 155 (no. 239). This treatise has not, to my knowledge, been the subject of close scholarly scrutiny. Louis Massignon mentioned it briefly in his *Essai sur les origines du lexique technique de la mystique musulmane* (Paris: J. Vrin, 1954), 254–55, as did Merlin Swartz in the introduction to his edition of Ibn al-Jawzī, *Kitāb al-quṣṣāṣ wa'l-mudhakkirīn,* 59n.

57. Swartz, *Ibn al-Jawzī's Kitāb al-Quṣṣāṣ,* 59n. The editor of al-Suyūṭī's *Taḥdhīr al-khawāṣṣ,* Muḥammad al-Ṣabbāgh, announced that he had prepared for publication a manuscript of al-ʿIrāqī's work, preserved in the library of the University of Riyadh; as far as I know, however, this edition has never appeared.

58. Biographical information is taken from Ibn Ḥajar al-ʿAsqalānī, *Inbā' al-ghumr,* 5:170–76; Ibn Taghrī Birdī, *al-Manhal al-ṣāfī,* 7:245–50; al-Sakhāwī, *al-Ḍaw' al-lāmiʿ,* 4:171–78; Ibn al-ʿImād, *Shadharāt al-dhahab,* 7:55–56.

59. al-Sakhāwī, *al-Ḍaw' al-lāmiʿ,* 4:175.

60. See, for example, ibid., 1:338.

61. B.L. Or 4275, fol. 4r.

62. Ibn Ḥajar, *al-Durar al-kāmina,* 5:49; al-Shaʿrānī, *al-Ṭabaqāt al-kubrā,* 2:19–20. There is some confusion over Ibn Wafā's date of death. Brockelmann,

GAL S II, 148, gives it as 760/1358. Ibn Ḥajar identifies it as 765/1364; al-Sakhāwī, however, noted that Ibn Ḥajar, in his biographical notice of Ibn Wafā's son ʿAlī, commented that "his father was pleased with him and gave him permission [*adhina lahu*] to speak to the people when he [ʿAlī] was less than twenty." Since Ibn Ḥajar had given 759/1357 as ʿAlī's date of birth (al-Shaʿrānī said it was 761/1359), al-Sakhāwī remarked simply that there was a contradiction and that God knew the truth of the matter (al-Sakhāwī, *al-Ḍaw' al-lāmiʿ,* 6:21).

63. Muḥammad b. ʿAbd al-Raḥmān al-Sakhāwī, *al-Tibr al-masbūk li-dhayl al-sulūk* (Cairo: Maktabat al-Kulliyāt al-Azhariyya, n.d.), 247–48.

64. J. Spencer Trimingham, *The Sufi Orders in Islam* (Oxford: Oxford University Press, 1971), 49, 87; F. De Jong, *Ṭuruq and Ṭuruq-Linked Institutions in Nineteenth-Century Egypt: A Historical Study in Organizational Dimensions of Islamic Mysticism* (Leiden: E. J. Brill, 1978), 76–77; Michael Winter, *Society and Religion in Early Ottoman Egypt: Studies in the Writings of ʿAbd al-Wahhāb al-Shaʿrānī* (New Brunswick, N.J.: Transaction Books, 1982), 130.

65. ʿAlī Pasha Mubārak, *al-Khiṭaṭ al-tawfīqiyya al-jadīda li-miṣr wa'l-qāhira,* 20 vols. (Būlāq: al-Maṭbaʿa al-Kubrā al-Amīriyya, 1305 A.H.), 5:138–39; Muḥammad Tawfīq al-Bakrī, *Kitāb bayt al-sādāt al-wafā'iyya* (Cairo, n.d.), 59–67.

66. On ʿAlī b. Muḥammad b. Wafā', see Ibn Ḥajar, *Inbā' al-ghumr,* 5:253–56; al-Sakhāwī, *al-Ḍaw' al-lāmiʿ,* 6:21–22; al-Shaʿrānī, *al-Ṭabaqāt al-kubrā,* 2:20–60; Ibn al-ʿImād, *Shadharat al-dhahab,* 7:70–72. There is a brief biography in a modern work: Muḥyī 'l-Dīn al-Ṭuʿmī, *Ṭabaqāt al-shādhiliyya al-kubrā* (Beirut: Dār al-Jīl, 1996), 183. Here, again, there is some disagreement regarding ʿAlī's date of death; al-Shaʿrānī gives it as 801.

67. Brockelmann, *GAL* 2:120, suppl. 2:149.

2 / STORYTELLING AND PREACHING IN THE LATE MIDDLE PERIOD

1. ʿAlī Pashā Mubārak, *al-Khiṭaṭ al-tawfīqiyya al-jadīda li-miṣr wa'l-qāhira,* 20 vols. (Būlāq: al-Maṭbaʿa al-Kubrā al-Amīriyya, 1305 A.H.), 5:138–39.

2. Ibn al-Ḥājj al-ʿAbdarī, *Madkhal al-sharʿ al-sharīf,* 4 vols. (Cairo: al-Maṭbaʿa al-Miṣriyya, 1929), 1:268.

3. Ibid., 2:12–16.

4. Huda Lutfi, "Manners and Customs of Fourteenth-Century Cairene Women: Female Anarchy versus Male Sharʿī Order in Muslim Prescriptive Treatises," in *Women in Middle Eastern History: Shifting Boundaries in Sex and Gender,* ed. Nikki Keddie and Beth Baron (New Haven: Yale University Press, 1991), 99–121.

5. On the cemeteries as a "liminal space," in which behavior that was unthinkable elsewhere became possible, see Christopher S. Taylor, *In the Vicinity of the Righteous: Ziyāra and the Veneration of Muslim Saints in Late Medieval Egypt* (Leiden: E. J. Brill, 1998).

6. Ibn al-Ḥājj, *Madkhal al-sharʿ al-sharīf,* 2:12–13.

7. Aḥmad b. ʿAlī al-Qalqashandī, *Ṣubḥ al-aʿshā fī ṣināʿat al-inshāʾ*, 14 vols. (Cairo: al-Muʾassasa al-Miṣriyya al-ʿĀmma liʾl-Taʾlīf waʾl-Tarjama waʾl-Ṭibāʿa waʾl-Nashr, 1964), 4:39; Carl Petry, *The Civilian Elite of Cairo in the Later Middle Ages* (Princeton: Princeton University Press, 1981), 260–61; Jonathan Berkey, *The Transmission of Knowledge in Medieval Cairo: A Social History of Islamic Education* (Princeton: Princeton University Press, 1992), 54–55, 194–96.

8. Discussed briefly in Berkey, *Transmission of Knowledge,* 206–10; see also George Makdisi, *The Rise of Colleges: Institutions of Learning in Islam and the West* (Edinburgh: Edinburgh University Press, 1981), 213.

9. Jalāl al-Dīn al-Suyūṭī, *Taḥdhīr al-khawāṣṣ min akādhib al-quṣṣāṣ,* ed. Muḥammad al-Sabbāgh (Beirut: al-Maktab al-Islāmī, 1972), 4.

10. Aḥmad b. ʿAlī al-Maqrīzī, *al-Sulūk li-maʿrifat duwal al-mulūk,* 4 vols. in 12, ed. Muḥammad Muṣṭafā Ziyāda and Saʿīd ʿAbd al-Fattāḥ ʿĀshūr (Cairo: Lajnat al-Taʾlīf waʾl-Tarjama waʾl-Nashr, 1956–73), 4:815–16; see also Muḥammad b. ʿAbd al-Raḥmān al-Sakhāwī, *al-Ḍawʾ al-lāmiʿ li-ahl al-qarn al-tāsiʿ,* 12 vols. (Cairo: Maktabat al-Qudsī, 1934), 2:50–51.

11. Khalīl b. Aybak al-Ṣafadī, *al-Wāfī biʾl-wafiyyāt,* 2d ed. (Wiesbaden: Franz Steiner Verlag, 1962–), 19:232–33.

12. al-Maqrīzī, *al-Sulūk,* 3:684.

13. al-Sakhāwī, *al-Ḍawʾ al-lāmiʿ,* 3:312–14.

14. Aḥmad b. Ḥajar al-ʿAsqalānī, *Inbāʾ al-ghumr bi-abnāʾ al-ʿumr,* 9 vols. (Haydarabad: Dāʾirat al-Maʿārif al-ʿUthmāniyya, 1967–76), 5:107–9.

15. Abū Bakr b. Aḥmad b. Qāḍī Shuhba, *Ṭabaqāt al-shāfiʿiyya,* 4 vols. (Haydarabad: Dāʾirat al-Maʿārif al-ʿUthmāniyya, 1979), 4:48, a loose translation of *wa qad khatama al-qurʾān al-ʿaẓīm bi-mīʿādihi wa atā fīhi min al-waʿẓ mā yakūnu in shaʾa allāh taʿālā shay*[an] *li-isʿādihi.*

16. al-Sakhāwī, *al-Ḍawʾ al-lāmiʿ,* 4:109, 112.

17. Cf. the remarks of Ignaz Goldziher, *Muslim Studies,* trans. C. R. Barber and S. M. Stern, 2 vols. (London: George Allen and Unwin, 1971), 2:153.

18. See the discussion of this literature by Camilla Adang, *Muslim Writers on Judaism and the Hebrew Bible from Ibn Rabban to Ibn Hazm* (Leiden: E. J. Brill, 1996), 8–16. Note in particular the confusion between the terms *qiṣaṣ al-anbiyāʾ* and *isrāʾīliyyāt;* ibid., 9.

19. See, for example, Wheeler M. Thackston Jr., *The Tales of the Prophets of al-Kisa'i* (Boston: Twayne Publishers, 1978), xv–xvi; see also Haim Schwarzbaum, *Biblical and Extra-Biblical Legends in Islamic Folk Literature* (Walldorf-Hessen: Verlag für Orientkunde Dr. H. Verndran, 1982), 39–45. Significantly, authors of more serious works of history may have included such tales, despite doubts about their historicity, because of their didactic value. See Tarif Khalidi, *Islamic Historiography: The Histories of Masʿūdī* (Albany: SUNY Press, 1975), 7, 43.

20. Ibn al-Jawzī, *Kitāb al-quṣṣāṣ wa'l-mudhakkirīn*, ed. Merlin Swartz (Beirut: Dar al-Machreq, 1986), 117 (Eng. trans., 202).

21. Jacob Lassner, *Demonizing the Queen of Sheba: Boundaries of Gender and Culture in Postbiblical Judaism and Medieval Islam* (Chicago: University of Chicago Press, 1993), 42–43; Reuven Firestone, *Journeys in Holy Lands: The Evolution of the Abraham-Ishmael Legends in Islamic Exegesis* (Albany: SUNY Press, 1990), 8.

22. M. J. Kister, "Ḥaddithū ʿan banī isrā'īla wa-lā ḥaraja: A Study of an Early Tradition," *Israel Oriental Studies* 2 (1972): 222–25; Hava Lazarus-Yafeh, *Intertwined Worlds: Medieval Islam and Bible Criticism* (Princeton: Princeton University Press, 1992), 75–110.

23. Steven M. Wasserstrom, *Between Muslim and Jew: The Problem of Symbiosis under Early Islam* (Princeton: Princeton University Press, 1995), 167–205, esp. 172–74. See also now Fred M. Donner, *Narratives of Islamic Origins: The Beginnings of Islamic Historical Writing* (Princeton: Darwin Press, 1998), 154–59.

24. Firestone, *Journeys*, 10, 13–14; Gordon Newby, "Tafsir Isra'iliyat: The Development of Qur'an Commentary in Early Islam in Its Relationship to Judaeo-Christian Traditions of Scriptural Commentary," in *Studies in Qur'an and Tafsir*, ed. Alford T. Welch, *Journal of the American Academy of Religion* 47, Thematic issue 4S (1980): 685–97. In fact, however, in the fluid religious context of the early medieval Near East, it is not always clear that Muslims simply borrowed these stories from Jews and Christians. On the contrary, there is much evidence of cultural cross-fertilization, as Muslims, Jews, and Christians, drawing on the stories and stock elements of a common tradition, shared their insights and knowledge. See Lassner, *Demonizing the Queen of Sheba*, 47, 123; Samuel Krauss, "A Moses Legend," *Jewish Quarterly Review*, n.s., 5 (1911–12): 339–64; Israel Friedlander, "A Muhammedan Book on Augury in Hebrew Characters," *Jewish Quarterly Review*, n.s., 19 (1917): 84–103; Joshua Finkel, "An Arabic Story of Abraham," *Hebrew Union College Annual* 12–13 (1938): 387–409. Suspicion of this extra-Qur'ānic material was associated with the crystallization of a more sharply defined Islamic identity, but the date of the shift is problematic. See Jane Dammen McAuliffe, "Assessing

the *Isrā'īliyyāt:* An Exegetical Conundrum," in *Story-telling in the Framework of Non-fictional Arabic Literature,* ed. Stefan Leder (Wiesbaden: Harrassowitz Verlag, 1998), 345–69, esp. 347–48 and 351 n.22.

25. Franz Rosenthal, *A History of Muslim Historiography* (Leiden: E. J. Brill, 1968), 335.

26. C. E. Bosworth, "Jewish Elements in the Banū Sāsān," *Bibliotheca Orientalis* 33 (1976): 292. Cf. McAuliffe, "Assessing the *Isrā'īliyyāt,*" 349–52.

27. William A. Graham, *Divine Word and Prophetic Word in Early Islam: A Reconsideration of the Sources, with Special Reference to the Divine Saying or Ḥadīth Qudsī* (The Hague: Mouton, 1977), 68–69.

28. Ibid., 83–84. This despite the reported remark of Ibn Ḥanbal that the *quṣṣāṣ* were "the most deceitful people"; see Ibn al-Ḥājj, *Madkhal al-sharʿ al-sharīf,* 2:146.

29. Ibn Taymiyya, *Aḥādīth al-quṣṣāṣ,* ed. Muḥammad al-Ṣabbāgh (Beirut: al-Maktab al-Islāmī, 1972), 69–70 (no. 3).

30. B.L. Or. 7528, fol. 32v–33v; cf. Mahmoud Ayoub, *The Qur'an and Its Interpreters* (Albany: SUNY Press, 1984), 1:265–66; ʿAbd Allāh b. ʿUmar al-Bayḍāwī, *Anwār al-tanzīl wa-asrār al-ta'wīl,* 2 vols. (Beirut: Dār al-Kutub al-ʿIlmiyya, 1988), 1:137; Ismāʿīl b. ʿUmar b. Kathīr, *Tafsīr al-qur'ān al-ʿaẓīm,* 4 vols. (Beirut: Dār al-Maʿrifa, 1995), 1:323.

31. Ibn Taymiyya, *Aḥādīth al-quṣṣāṣ,* 72–73 (no. 6).

32. Ibid., 87 (no. 29).

33. Ibid., 89 (no. 33).

34. The story is found in the Qur'ān, 37:100–7; there the son in question is not named. Muslim historians and commentators in fact disagreed about whether Isaac or Ishmael was intended for the sacrifice. Cf. Firestone, *Journeys in Holy Lands,* 135–51; *EI* 2d ed., art. "ISḤĀQ" (by W. Montgomery Watt); and "ISMĀʿĪL" (by Rudi Paret).

35. B.L. Or. 7528, fol. 33v–35r.

36. Ibid., fol. 37v–39r.

37. Ibid., fol. 35r.

38. Ibn Taymiyya, *Aḥādīth al-quṣṣāṣ,* 117 (no. 76).

39. Ibid., 112–13 (no. 69).

40. Ibid., 78, 81–82 (nos. 15, 18).

41. Ibid., 77–78, 86–87 (nos. 14, 28).

42. Ibid., 84–85, 113 (nos. 22–24, 70).

43. Ibid., 111 (no. 65).

44. Ibid., (no. 66).

45. Ibid., 88 (nos. 30, 31).

46. Ibid., 112 (no. 68).

47. Ibid., 109 (no. 63). Note the pun in this hadith: Egypt was frequently referred to as *arḍ al-kināna,* "the land of the Kināna tribe."

48. Ibid., 74 (no. 7).

49. Ibid., 84 (no. 21).

50. Ibid., 92 (no. 37).

51. Ibid., 75–76 (nos. 11–12). Cf. a story in B.L. Or. 7528, fol. 61v–63r, and another about Jesus in fol. 55r.

52. ʿAbd Allāh b. Saʿd Allāh al-Ḥurayfish, *al-Rawḍ al-fāʾiq fiʾl-mawāʿiẓ waʾl-raqāʾiq* (Cairo: Muṣṭafā al-Bābī al-Ḥalabī, 1949), 67–68.

53. Ibn Taymiyya, *Aḥādīth al-quṣṣāṣ,* 79 (no. 16).

54. B.L. Or. 7528, fol. 19r–v.

55. Ibn Taymiyya, *Aḥādīth al-quṣṣāṣ,* 93 (no. 39).

56. Ibid., 106 (no. 57).

57. Ibid., 109–11 (no. 64).

58. Ibid., 95–96 (no. 42). See Louis Massignon, *The Passion of al-Ḥallāj: Mystic and Martyr of Islam,* trans. Herbert Mason, 4 vols. (Princeton: Princeton University Press, 1982), 2:14–15.

59. Ibn Taymiyya, *Aḥādīth al-quṣṣāṣ,* 118 (no. 79).

60. Ibid., 92 (no. 36).

61. Ibid., 116 (no. 74).

62. See, for example, Boaz Shoshan's remarks concerning popular religion in medieval Cairo, *Popular Culture in Medieval Cairo* (Cambridge: Cambridge University Press, 1993), 4–6. Abū Ḥāmid al-Ghazālī devoted an entire book of his monumental *Iḥyāʾ ʿulūm al-dīn* to "the remembrance of death and what follows it." *Iḥyāʾ ʿulūm al-dīn,* 5 vols. (Cairo: al-Ḥalabī, 1968), 4:556–680; trans. T. J. Winter, *The Remembrance of Death and the Afterlife* (Cambridge: Islamic Texts Society, 1989).

63. A full-scale study of Islamic asceticism remains a desideratum; for now, see Leah Kinberg, "What Is Meant by *Zuhd?*" *Studia Islamica* 61 (1985): 27–44; Ahmet Karamustafa, *God's Unruly Friends: Dervish Groups in the Islamic Later Middle Period, 1200–1550* (Salt Lake City: University of Utah Press, 1994), 25–30.

64. Qāsim b. ʿAlī al-Ḥarīrī, *Maqāmāt* (Beirut: Dār Ṣādir, 1980), 16–21; trans. T. Chenery, *The Assemblies of al-Ḥarīrī* (London: Williams and Northgate, 1867), 1:109–11; trans. F. Steinglass, *The Assemblies of al-Ḥarīrī* (London: S. Low, Marston, 1898), 2:109–11. See also David Pinault, *Story-telling Techniques in the Arabian Nights* (Leiden: E. J. Brill, 1992), 231–37.

65. ʿAbd al-Raḥmān b. ʿAlī b. al-Jawzī, *al-Yāqūta fiʾl-waʿẓ* (Cairo: ʿĪsā Bābī al-Ḥalabī, 1351 A.H.), 37–38.

66. B.L. Or. 7528, fol. 22r–v.

67. al-Ḥurayfīsh, *al-Rawḍ al-fā'iq,* 60–66.

68. Ibid., 64. The collections of the *qiṣaṣ al-anbiyā'* record many such tales about Adam: see, for example, Ismā'īl b. 'Umar b. Kathīr, *Qiṣaṣ al-anbiyā',* ed. 'Abd al-Mu'ṭī 'Abd al-Maqṣūd Muḥammad (Alexandria: Maktabat Ḥamīdū, 1990), 24; Aḥmad b. Muḥammad al-Tha'labī, *Qiṣaṣ al-anbiyā' al-musammā bi'l-'arā'is* (Cairo: Maktabat al-Jumhūriyya al-'Arabiyya, n.d.), 21; and Wheeler Thackston Jr., *The Tales of the Prophets of al-Kisā'ī* (Boston: Twayne Publishers, 1978), esp. 55–59.

69. al-Ḥurayfish, *al-Rawḍ al-fā'iq,* 61, 62, 65.

70. Ibid., 62–63.

71. Ibid., 62.

72. Ibid., 263.

73. Ibid., 90. See also al-Tha'labī, *Qiṣaṣ al-anbiyā',* 35, 218; Ibn Kathīr, *Qiṣaṣ al-anbiyā',* 97, 672; Thackston, *Tales of the Prophets,* 333–34.

74. al-Ḥurayfish, *al-Rawḍ al-fā'iq,* 89–93.

75. Ibid., 17.

76. Ibid., 264.

77. Ibn al-Jawzī, *Kitāb al-quṣṣāṣ wa'l-mudhakkirīn,* 141–42 (Eng. trans., 225–26).

78. al-Ḥurayfish, *al-Rawḍ al-fā'iq,* 39–40.

79. 'Abd al-Wahhāb al-Sha'rānī, *al-Ṭabaqāt al-kubrā,* 2 vols. (Cairo: Muḥammad 'Alī Ṣubayḥ, 1965), 1:177; see also Tāj al-Dīn 'Abd al-Wahhāb al-Subkī, *Ṭabaqāt al-shāfi'iyya al-kubrā,* 2d ed., 10 vols., ed. 'Abd al-Fattāḥ Muḥammad al-Hilw and Maḥmūd Muḥammad al-Ṭanāhī (Cairo: Hajar, 1992), 8:123–24; and Muḥammad b. 'Abd al-Raḥīm b. al-Furāt, *Tārīkh,* ed. Qusṭanṭīn Zurayq and Najlā 'Izz al-Dīn, vols. 7–9 (Beirut: American University in Beirut Press, 1938), 8:72–73.

80. Shoshan, *Popular Culture in Medieval Cairo,* 9–22; Th. Emil Homerin, "Sufis and Their Detractors in Mamluk Egypt: A Survey of Protagonists and Institutional Settings," in *Islamic Mysticism Contested: Thirteen Centuries of Controversies and Polemics,* ed. Frederick De Jong and Bernd Radtke (Leiden: Brill, 1999), 225–47.

81. 'Abd al-Raḥmān b. 'Alī b. al-Jawzī, *al-Muntaẓam fī tārīkh al-mulūk wa'l-umam,* 10 vols. (Haydarabad: Dā'irat al-Ma'ārif al-'Uthmāniyya, 1359 A.H.), 8:76.

82. Swartz, *Ibn al-Jawzī's Kitāb al-Quṣṣāṣ,* 23–25, 62.

83. Ibn al-Jawzī, *al-Muntaẓam,* 9:260–62. See also Aḥmad b. Muḥammad b. Khallikān, *Wafayāt al-a'yān wa anbā' abnā' al-zamān,* ed. Iḥsān 'Abbās, 8 vols. (Beirut: Dār Ṣādir, 1978), 1:97, trans. MacGuckin de Slane, *Ibn Khallikan's*

Biographical Dictionary, 4 vols. (Paris: Oriental Translation Fund of Great Britain and Ireland, 1842), 1:79, according to whom Aḥmad al-Ghazālī's preoccupation with preaching led him to neglect the study of jurisprudence. On the Sufi understanding and defense of Satan, see Peter J. Awn, *Satan's Tragedy and Redemption: Iblīs in Sufi Psychology* (Leiden: E. J. Brill, 1983).

84. Jean-Claude Garcin, "Histoire, opposition politique et piétisme traditionaliste dans le *Ḥusn al-Muḥādarat* de Suyūṭī," *Annales Islamologiques* 7 (1967): 81–82.

85. al-Sakhāwī, *al-Ḍaw' al-lāmiʿ,* 2:188–90.

86. Ibn al-Jawzī, *Kitāb al-quṣṣāṣ wa'l-mudhakkirīn,* 115 (Eng. trans., 199–200).

87. See also Th. Emil Homerin, "Preaching Poetry: The Forgotten Verse of Ibn al-Shahrazūrī," *Arabica* 38 (1991): 87–88.

88. Ibn al-Jawzī, *Kitāb al-quṣṣāṣ wa'l-mudhakkirīn,* 117 (Eng. trans., 202). And, indeed, B.L. Or. 7528 includes a defense of al-Ḥallāj: see fol. 112r–113r.

89. al-Sakhāwī, *al-Ḍaw' al-lāmiʿ,* 5:20.

90. Aḥmad b. Ḥajar al-ʿAsqalānī, *al-Durar al-kāmina fī aʿyān al-mi'a al-thāmina,* ed. Muḥammad Sayyid Jād al-Ḥaqq, 5 vols. (Cairo: Dār al-Kutub al-Ḥadītha, 1966–67), 3:420–21; al-Maqrīzī, *al-Sulūk,* 2:408; al-Subkī, *Ṭabaqāt al-shāfiʿiyya,* 9:94–96; Jean Claude Vadet, "Les Idées d'un prédicateur de mosquée au XIVᵉ siècle dans le Caire des Mamlouks," *Annales Islamologiques* 8 (1969): 63–69.

91. *al-Bāʿithʿ alā'l-khalāṣ,* fol. 23v–24r.

3 / THE SOCIAL AND POLITICAL CONTEXT OF PREACHING

1. ʿAbd al-Raḥmān b. ʿAlī b. al-Jawzī, *al-Muntaẓam fī tārīkh al-mulūk wa'l-umam,* 10 vols. (Haydarabad: Dā'irat al-Maʿārif al-ʿUthmāniyya, 1359 A.H.), 9:75–76; Abū'l-Muẓaffar Yūsuf Sibṭ b. al-Jawzī, *Mirāt al-zamān fī tārīkh al-aʿyān,* vol. 8 in 2 (Haydarabad: Dā'irat al-Maʿārif al-ʿUthmāniyya, 1951–52), 1:5.

2. Abū Bakr Aḥmad b. ʿAlī al-Khaṭīb al-Baghdādī, *Tārīkh baghdād,* 14 vols. (Beirut: Dār al-Kitāb al-ʿArabī, 1966), 1:359–60.

3. Peter Heath makes a similar point regarding public performances of epic narratives such as the *Sīrat ʿAntar,* in *The Thirsty Sword: Sīrat ʿAntar and the Arabic Popular Epic* (Salt Lake City: University of Utah Press, 1996), 41. See also Boaz Shoshan, "On Popular Literature in Medieval Cairo," *Poetics Today* 14 (1993): 349–65, esp. 351.

4. Muḥammad b. Aḥmad b. Jubayr, *Riḥla* (Beirut: Dār Ṣādir, 1980), 195, 198.

5. B.L.Or. 7528, fol. 33v–35r.

6. Ibid., fol. 44v–47r.

7. Ibid., fol. 47v–48r.

8. Jonathan P. Berkey, "Tradition, Innovation, and the Social Construction of Knowledge in the Medieval Islamic Near East," *Past and Present* 146 (1995): 38–65.

9. ʿAlī b. Wafāʾ, *al-Bāʿith ʿalā'l-khalāṣ min sūʾ al-ẓann biʾl-khawāṣṣ,* B.L. Or. 4275, fol. 11r–12v.

10. Muḥammad b. ʿAbd al-Raḥmān al-Sakhāwī, *al-Ḍawʾ al-lāmiʿ li-ahl al-qarn al-tāsiʿ,* 12 vols. (Cairo: Maktabat al-Qudsī, 1934), 2:9–11.

11. Khalil ʿAthamina, "Al-Qasas: Its Emergence, Religious Origin and Its Socio-political Impact on Early Muslim Society," *Studia Islamica* 76 (1992): 65–74.

12. ʿAbd al-Raḥmān b. ʿAlī b. al-Jawzī, *Kitāb al-quṣṣāṣ waʾl-mudhakkirīn,* ed. Merlin L. Swartz (Beirut: Dar el-Machreq, 1986), 28–29 (Eng. trans., 114–15).

13. Bernard Lewis, "The Significance of Heresy in Islam," *Studia Islamica* 1 (1953): 43–63; Alexander Knysh, "'Orthodoxy' and 'Heresy' in Medieval Islam: An Essay in Reassessment," *Muslim World* 83 (1993): 48–67.

14. See *EI,* 2d ed., art. "MIḤNA" (by M. Hinds). In their book *God's Caliph: Religious Authority in the First Centuries of Islam* (Cambridge: Cambridge University Press, 1986), Patricia Crone and Martin Hinds have suggested that the early Islamic caliphs in fact conceived of their office as the principal locus of religious and legal authority. In this analysis they have recast the historical significance of the *miḥna* as representing the final significant effort to give practical effect to this caliphal authority, its failure marking the definitive passing of religious and legal authority to the ulama. See *God's Caliph,* esp. 94–96. In any case, by the Islamic Middle Period religious authority was defined through consensus, rather than institutions.

15. On this point, see Berkey, "Tradition, Innovation, and the Social Construction of Knowledge."

16. Th. Emil Homerin, *From Arab Poet to Muslim Saint: Ibn al-Fāriḍ, His Verse, and His Shrine* (Columbia: University of South Carolina Press, 1994), 55–75, esp. 69–75.

17. ʿAlī b. Wafāʾ, *al-Bāʿith ʿalā'l-khalāṣ,* fol. 4r–v.

18. Ibid., fol. 4v–6r.

19. Ibid., fol. 10r–11r. See also Ibn al-Jawzī, *Kitāb al-quṣṣāṣ waʾl-mudhakkirīn,* 37, 127 (Eng. trans., 122–23, 211); and M. J. Kister, "Ḥaddithū ʿan banī isrāʾīla wa-lā ḥaraja: A Study of an Early Tradition," *Israel Oriental Studies* 2 (1972): 232.

20. ʿAlī ibn Wafāʾ, *al-Bāʿith ʿalā'l-khalāṣ,* fol. 6r–10r.

21. George Makdisi, *Ibn ʿAqīl et la résurgence de l'Islam traditionaliste au XI*[e] *siècle (V*[e] *siècle de l'Hégire)* (Damascus: Institut Français de Damas, 1963), esp. 340–75.

22. See, for example, an incident that occurred in 475/1082–83, as reported by ʿAlī b. Muḥammad b. al-Athīr, *al-Kāmil fi'l-tārīkh,* ed. Yūsuf al-Daqqāq, 10 vols. (Beirut: Dār al-Kutub al-ʿIlmiyya, 1995), 8:428; cf. George Makdisi, *The Rise of Colleges: Institutions of Learning in Islam and the West* (Edinburgh: Edinburgh University Press, 1981), 15–16; and idem, "Muslim Institutions of Learning in Eleventh-Century Baghdad," *BSOAS* 24 (1961): 46–47.

23. Emmanuel Sivan, *L'Islam et la croisade: Idéologie et propagande dans les réactions musulmane aux croisades* (Paris: Librairie d'Amérique et d'Orient, 1968), 68–69.

24. ʿAbd al-Raḥmān b. Aḥmad b. Rajab, *Kitāb al-dhayl ʿalā ṭabaqāt al-ḥanābila,* ed. Muḥammad Ḥāmid al-Fiqī, 2 vols. (Cairo: Maktabat al-Sunna al-Muḥammadiyya, 1952–53), 1:370.

25. Sivan, *L'Islam et la croisade,* 41–43.

26. Makdisi, *Ibn ʿAqīl et la résurgence de l'Islam traditionaliste,* 350–66.

27. Sibṭ b. al-Jawzī, *Mir'āt al-zamān,* 1:126, 183–84; Tāj al-Dīn ʿAbd al-Wahhāb al-Subkī, *Tabaqāt al-shāfiʿiyya al-kubrā,* 2d ed., 10 vols., ed. ʿAbd al-Fattāḥ Muḥammad al-Hilw and Maḥmūd Muḥammad al-Ṭanāhī (Cairo: Hajar, 1992), 6:178.

28. Sibṭ b. al-Jawzī, *Mir'āt al-zamān,* 2:443–44.

29. Aḥmad b. Muḥammad b. Khallikān, *Wafayāt al-aʿyān wa anbā' abnā' al-zamān,* ed. Iḥsān ʿAbbās, 8 vols. (Beirut: Dār Ṣādir, 1978), 5:212–13, trans. MacGuckin de Slane, *Ibn Khallikān's Biographical Dictionary,* 4 vols. (Paris: Oriental Translation Fund of Great Britain and Ireland, 1842), 3:365–66; Ibn al-Jawzī, *al-Muntaẓam,* 10:150–51.

30. Sibṭ b. al-Jawzī, *Mir'āt al-zamān,* 2:515.

31. Aḥmad b. Ḥajar al-ʿAsqalānī, *Inbā' al-ghumr bi-abnā' al-ʿumr,* 9 vols. (Haydarabad: Dā'irat al-Maʿārif al-ʿUthmāniyya, 1967–76), 9:15–165; Abū'l-Maḥāsin Yūsuf b. Taghrī Birdī, *al-Manhal al-ṣāfī wa'l-mustawfī baʿd al-wāfī,* ed. Muḥammad M. Amīn, 7 vols. to date (Cairo: al-Hay'a al-Miṣriyya al-ʿĀmma li'l-Kitāb, 1984–) 2:78; al-Sakhāwī, *al-Ḍaw' al-lāmiʿ,* 2:142; ʿAbd al-Ḥayy b. Aḥmad b. al-ʿImād, *Shadharāt al-dhahab fī akhbār man dhahab,* 8 vols. (Cairo: Maktabat al-Qudsī, 1931–32), 7:238.

32. In the very different circumstances of late twentieth-century Saudi Arabia, the preaching tradition continues to provide a channel for religious criticism of political rulers. See Talal Asad, *Genealogies of Religion: Discipline and Reasons of Power in Christianity and Islam* (Baltimore: The Johns Hopkins University Press, 1993), 213–23.

33. Ibn al-Jawzī, *al-Muntaẓam,* 8:88–89; Adam Mez, *The Renaissance of Islam,*

trans. Salahuddin Khuda Bukhsh and D. S. Margoliouth (New York: AMS Press, 1975), 330–31.

34. Ibn al-Jawzī, *al-Muntaẓam,* 9:173–74.

35. Ibid., 8:87.

36. ʿAbd al-Raḥmān b. ʿAlī b. al-Jawzī, *Ṣayd al-khāṭir,* ed. Adam Abū Sunayna (Amman: Maktabat Dār al-Fikr, 1987), 409–10.

37. al-Subkī, *Ṭabaqāt al-shāfiʿiyya al-kubrā,* 8:209–55; Abū Bakr b. Aḥmad b. Qāḍī Shuhba, *Ṭabaqāt al-shāfiʿiyya,* 4 vols. (Haydarabad: Dā'irat al-Maʿārif al-ʿUthmāniyya, 1979) 2:138; Ismāʿīl b. ʿUmar b. Kathīr, *al-Bidāya wa'l-nihāya,* 14 vols. (Cairo: Maṭbaʿat al-Saʿāda, 1932–39), 13:235–36; R. Stephen Humphreys, *From Saladin to the Mongols: The Ayyubids of Damascus, 1193–1260* (Albany: SUNY Press, 1977), 267; Sivan, *L'Islam et la croisade,* 149–52.

38. Ibn Ḥajar, *Inbā' al-ghumr,* 7:232–33; Ibn Qāḍī Shuhba, *Ṭabaqāt al-shāfiʿiyya,* 4:31–33; Ibn Taghrī Birdī, *al-Manhal al-ṣāfī,* 7:223–24; al-Sakhāwī, *al-Ḍaw' al-lāmiʿ,* 4:140–42.

39. ʿAbd al-Wahhāb al-Shaʿrānī, *al-Ṭabaqāt al-kubrā,* 2 vols. (Cairo: Muḥammad ʿAlī Ṣubayḥ, 1965), 2:164–65.

40. ʿAbd al-Wahhāb al-Shaʿrānī, *al-Ṭabaqāt al-ṣughrā,* ed. ʿAbd al-Qādir Aḥmad ʿAṭā (Cairo: Maktabat al-Qāhira, 1970), 42.

41. Qāsim b. ʿAlī al-Ḥarīrī, *Maqāmāt* (Beirut: Dār Ṣādir, 1980), 16–21, trans. T. Chenery, *The Assemblies of al-Ḥarīrī* (London: Williams and Northgate, 1867), 1:109–11.

42. Khalīl b. Aybak al-Ṣafadī, *al-Wāfī bi'l-wafiyyāt,* 2d ed. (Wiesbaden: Franz Steiner Verlag, 1962–), 22:333–34.

43. al-Sakhāwī, *al-Ḍaw' al-lāmiʿ,* 2:50–51; Aḥmad b. ʿAlī al-Maqrīzī, *al-Sulūk li-maʿrifat duwal al-mulūk,* 4 vols. in 12, ed. Muḥammad Muṣṭafā Ziyāda and Saʿīd ʿAbd al-Fattāḥ ʿĀshūr (Cairo: Lajnat al-Ta'līf wa'l-Tarjama wa'l-Nashr, 1956–73), 4:815–16.

44. Jalāl al-Dīn al-Suyūṭī, *Taḥdhīr al-khawāṣṣ min akādhīb al-quṣṣāṣ,* ed. Muḥammad al-Sabbāgh (Beirut: al-Maktab al-Islāmī, 1972), 198.

45. Ibid., 109–38.

46. C. E. Bosworth, *The Medieval Islamic Underground: The Banū Ṣāsān in Arabic Society and Literature* (Leiden: E. J. Brill, 1976), 28.

47. Makdisi, *Ibn ʿAqīl et la résurgence de l'Islam traditionaliste,* 419–20.

48. Sibṭ b. al-Jawzī, *Mir'āt al-zamān,* 2:474–75.

49. Ḍiyā' al-Dīn Muḥammad b. al-Ukhuwwa, *Maʿālim al-qurba fī aḥkām al-ḥisba,* ed. Reuben Levy (E. J. W. Gibb Memorial Series, n.s., 12) (Cambridge: Cambridge University Press, 1938), 179.

50. Aḥmad b. ʿAlī al-Qalqashandi, *Ṣubḥ al-aʿshā fī ṣināʿat al-inshā',* 14 vols. (Cairo: al-Mu'assasa al-Miṣriyya al-ʿĀmma li'l-Ta'līf wa'l-Tarjama wa'l-Ṭibāʿa wa'l-Nashr, 1964), 4:39.

51. Ibn al-Jawzī, *al-Muntaẓam,* 10:166–68.

52. al-Shaʿrānī, *al-Ṭabaqāt al-kubrā,* 1:177.

53. al-Subkī, *Ṭabaqāt al-shāfiʿiyya,* 8:123–24.

54. al-Shaʿrānī, *al-Ṭabaqāt al-kubrā,* 2:2.

55. Aḥmad b. Ḥajar al-ʿAsqalānī, *al-Durar al-kāmina fī aʿyān al-mi'a al-thāmina,* ed. Muḥammad Sayyid Jād al-Ḥaqq, 5 vols. (Cairo: Dār al-Kutub al-Ḥadītha, 1966–67), 3:420–21; al-Maqrīzī, *al-Sulūk,* 2:408. For another example, see Ibn Taghrī Birdī, *al-Manhal al-ṣāfī,* 1:184–85.

56. Ibn Ḥajar, *Inbā' al-ghumr,* 4:91–92; al-Sakhawī, *al-Ḍaw' al-lāmiʿ,* 10:113–14. Ibn Ḥajar and, following him, al-Sakhāwī give his *shaykh*'s name as Ḥusayn al-Ḥabbār; that may, however, be a scribal error, for the individual intended is clearly the same whom most sources name al-Khabbāz. See ʿAlī b. Dā'ūd b. al-Ṣayrafi al-Jawharī, *Nuzhat al-nufūs wa'l-abdān fī tawārīkh al-zamān,* ed. Ḥasan Ḥabashī, 4 vols. (Cairo: Wizārat al-Thaqāfa, 1970–), 1:277; al-Maqrīzī, *al-Sulūk,* 3:685–86; Abū'l-Maḥāsin Yūsuf b. Taghrī Birdī, *al-Nujūm al-zāhira fī mulūk miṣr wa'l-qāhira,* 16 vols. (Cairo: al-Mu'assasa al-Miṣriyya al-ʿĀmma li'l-Ta'līf wa'l-Ṭibāʿa wa'l-Nashr, 1963–71) 11:385. Muḥammad b. ʿAbd al-Raḥīm b. al-Furāt, *Tārīkh,* ed. Qusṭanṭīn Zurayq and Najlā ʿIzz al-Dīn, vols. 7–9 (Beirut: American University in Beirut Press, 1938), 9:173–74, however, named him al-Ḥabbār. There seems also to have been confusion about whether his name was Ḥasan or Ḥusayn.

57. ʿAlī b. Wafā', *al-Bāʿith ʿalā'l-khalāṣ,* 11r–12v.

58. al-Sakhāwī, *al-Ḍaw' al-lāmiʿ,* 4:296–97.

59. al-Ḥurayfish, *al-Rawḍ al-fā'iq,* 67.

60. Ibid., 73.

61. B.L. Or. 7528, fol. 56v.

4 / STORYTELLING, PREACHING, AND KNOWLEDGE

1. Ibn al-Ḥājj al-ʿAbdarī, *Madkhal al-sharʿ al-sharīf,* 4 vols. (Cairo: al-Maṭbaʿa al-Miṣriyya, 1929), 1:89. For a general discussion of the importance of knowledge to the Islamic tradition, see Franz Rosenthal, *Knowledge Triumphant: The Concept of Knowledge in Medieval Islam* (Leiden: E. J. Brill, 1970). An excellent recent study of the social uses of religious knowledge can be found in Michael Chamberlain, *Knowledge and Social Practice in Medieval Damascus, 1190–1350* (Cambridge: Cambridge University Press, 1994). Patrick Gaffney discusses the

relationship between knowledge and authority in a contemporary Islamic society in *The Prophet's Pulpit: Islamic Preaching in Contemporary Egypt* (Berkeley: University of California Press, 1994), esp. 34–36.

2. Michael Gilsenan, *Recognizing Islam: Religion and Society in the Modern Middle East* (London: I. B. Tauris, 1992), 36. More generally, see Gilsenan's discussion of the textual character of Islamic authority and its mediation through the ulama (ibid., 30–36).

3. On the flexibility of medieval definitions of what constituted *ʿilm,* see Jonathan P. Berkey, "Tradition, Innovation, and the Social Construction of Knowledge in the Medieval Islamic Near East," *Past and Present* 146 (1995): 38–65.

4. Ibn al-Ḥājj, *Madkhal al-sharʿ al-sharīf,* 2:144.

5. ʿAlī b. Wafāʾ, *al-Bāʿith ʿalāʾl-khalāṣ min sūʾ al-ẓann biʾl-khawāṣṣ,* B.L. Or. 4275, fol. 12v–15v, esp. 13v.

6. Ibid., fol. 22v.

7. ʿAbd al-Raḥmān b. ʿAlī b. al-Jawzī, *Kitāb al-quṣṣāṣ wa ʾl-mudhakkirīn,* ed. Merlin Swartz (Beirut: Dar al-Machreq, 1986), 108 (Eng. trans., 191–92); cited in Jalāl al-Dīn al-Suyūṭī, *Taḥdhīr al-khawāṣṣ min akādhīb al-quṣṣāṣ,* ed. Muhammad al-Sabbāgh (Beirut: al-Maktab al-Islāmī, 1972), 230.

8. Cf., for example, Ṭāj al-Dīn ʿAbd al-Wahhāb al-Subkī's defense of the *wāʿiẓ* Muḥammad b. Muḥammad al-Khuzaymī, in *Ṭabaqāt al-shāfiʿiyya al-kubrā,* 2d ed., 10 vols., ed. ʿAbd al-Fattāḥ Muḥammad al-Hilw and Maḥmūd Muḥammad al-Ṭanāhī (Cairo: Hajar, 1992), 6:190–91, in the face of criticism by Ibn al-Jawzī, *al-Muntaẓam fī tārīkh al-mulūk wa ʾl-umam,* 10 vols. (Haydarabad: Dāʾirat al-Maʿārif al-ʿUthmāniyya, 1359 A.H.), 9:221–22.

9. al-Suyūṭī, *Taḥdhīr al-khawāṣṣ,* 155. It should hardly be surprising that there might exist a direct correlation between the popularity of a hadīth with the common people and the danger that it was false. Consider, for example, a comment recorded by Abūʾl-Qāsim al-Balkhī: "Show me the biggest liar, for the best traditions can only be found with him." Cited in G. H. A. Juynboll, *Muslim Tradition: Studies in Chronology, Provenance, and Authorship of Early Ḥadīth* (Cambridge: Cambridge University Press, 1983), 133.

10. Aḥmad b. Taymiyya, *Aḥādīth al-quṣṣāṣ,* ed. Muḥammad al-Ṣabbāgh (Beirut: al-Maktab al-Islāmī, 1972), 83 (no.20).

11. Ibid., 78 (no. 15). See also Muḥammad b. ʿAbd al-Raḥmān al-Sakhāwī, *al-Maqāṣid al-ḥasana fī bayān kathīr min al-aḥādīth al-mushtahara ʿalāʾl-alsina,* ed. ʿAbd Allāh Muḥammad al-Ṣadīq (Cairo: al-Khāngī, 1991), 97–98. This tradition is also recorded in B.L. Or. 7528, in a context that clearly indicates that it was popular with Sunnis as well as Shīʿīs; see fol. 56v–57v.

12. Ibn Taymiyya, *Aḥādīth al-quṣṣāṣ,* 74 (no. 7).

13. Ibid., 104 (no. 54).

14. ʿAlī b. Wafāʾ, *al-Bāʿith ʿalā ʾl-khalāṣ,* fol. 15v. Not all sources agreed about al-Raqāshī's credentials. Al-Jāḥiẓ, for one, considered him an excellent preacher and storyteller and noted that he was a companion of Ḥasan al-Baṣrī. See *al-Bayān wa ʾl-tabyīn,* ed. ʿAbd al-Salām Muḥammad Hārūn, 4 vols. (Cairo: al-Khāngī, 1968), 1:308; and Charles Pellat, *Le Milieu baṣrien et la formation de Ǧāḥiẓ* (Paris: Librairie d'Amérique et d'Orient, 1953), 113.

15. ʿAlī b. Wafāʾ, *al-Bāʿith ʿalā ʾl-khalāṣ,* fol. 15v–16v.

16. Quoted in al-Suyūṭī, *Taḥdhīr al-khawāṣṣ,* 108; see also ʿAlī b. Wafāʾ, *al-Bāʿith ʿalā ʾl-khalāṣ,* fol. 25v.

17. Ibn al-Ḥājj *Madkhal al-sharʿ al-sharīf,* 2:218–19.

18. al-ʿIrāqī, quoted in ʿAlī b. Wafāʾ, *al-Bāʿith ʿalā ʾl-khalāṣ,* fol. 24r.

19. al-Suyūṭī, *Taḥdhīr al-khawāṣṣ,* 179–80.

20. Ibid., 8–66.

21. Ibid., 5.

22. Ibid., 92.

23. Ibid., 90–91.

24. ʿAlī b. Wafāʾ, *al-Bāʿith ʿalā ʾl-khalāṣ,* fol. 26r–27r. The leading medieval authority on the transmission of hadith considered *riwāyat al-wijāda* among the least respectable modes of transmission (Ibn al-Ṣalāḥ al-Shahrazūrī, *ʿUlūm al-ḥadīth,* ed. Nūr al-Dīn ʿAtar [Beirut: Dār al-Fikr, 1984], 178–81).

25. al-Suyūṭī, *Taḥdhīr al-khawāṣṣ,* 70, citing Muḥyī ʾl-Dīn Abū Zakariyyā al-Nawawī, *Sharḥ ṣaḥīḥ muslim,* 18 vols. in 6 (Beirut: Muʾassasat Manāhil al-ʿIrfān, n.d.), 1:70.

26. Ibn ʿAdī, quoted in al-Suyūṭī, *Taḥdhīr al-khawāṣṣ,* 71–73.

27. Ibn al-Ṣalāh, *ʿUlūm al-ḥadīth,* 98–99, quoted in al-Suyūṭī, *Taḥdhīr al-khawāṣṣ,* 73. Historians, too, adopted less critical standards in judging reports drawn from sources such as the Isrāʾīliyyāt, if such reports had a didactic value. See Tarif Khalidi, *Islamic Historiography: The Histories of Masʿūdī* (Albany: SUNY Press, 1975), 43.

28. al-Suyūṭī, *Taḥdhīr al-khawāṣṣ,* 73–75; see also Ignaz Goldziher, *Muslim Studies,* trans. S. M. Stern and C. M. Barber (London: George Allen and Unwin, 1971), 2:145–48.

29. Boaz Shoshan, *Popular Culture in Medieval Cairo* (Cambridge: Cambridge University Press, 1993), 14.

30. Ibn al-Jawzī, *Kitāb al-quṣṣāṣ wa ʾl-mudhakkirīn,* 142 (Eng. trans., 226–28).

31. Ibn al-Ḥājj, *Madkhal al-sharʿ al-sharīf,* 2:147–53.

32. Ibn Taymiyya, *Aḥādīth al-quṣṣāṣ,* 72–73.

33. See, for example, al-Ḥurayfīsh, *al-Rawḍ al-fā'iq,* 11, 28.

34. ʿAlī b. Wafā', *al-Bāʿith ʿalā'l-khalāṣ,* fol. 27r–v.

35. This story is well attested in the standard heresiographies; see, for example, ʿAbd al-Qāhir b. Ṭāhir al-Baghdādī, *al-Farq bayna 'l-firaq,* ed. Ṭaha ʿAbd al-Ra'ūf Saʿd (Cairo: al-Halabī, n.d.), 71; and Muḥammad b. ʿAbd al-Karīm al-Shahrastānī, *Kitāb al-milal wa 'l-niḥal,* ed. ʿAbd al-ʿAzīz Muḥammad al-Wakīl, 3 vols. (Cairo: al-Ḥalabī, n.d.), 1:48, trans. A. K. Kazi and J. G. Flynn, *Muslim Sects and Divisions* (London: Kegan Paul, 1984), 44–45.

36. B.L. Or. 7528, fol. 102v–105r.

37. ʿAlī b. Wafā', *al-Bāʿith ʿalā'l-khalāṣ,* fol. 18v. Massignon gave a truncated synopsis of this exchange, in *Essai sur les origines du lexique technique de la mystique musulmane* (Paris: J. Vrin, 1954), 254–55.

38. Muhsin Mahdi, *Ibn Khaldūn's Philosophy of History* (Chicago: University of Chicago Press, 1964), 63–73.

39. Qur'ān 12.111 and 79.26. For other occurrences, see 3.13, 16.66, 23.21, and 24.44. See also Muḥammad Fu'ād ʿAbd al-Bāqī, *al-Muʿjam al-mufahras li-alfāẓ al-qur'ān al-karīm* (Cairo: Dār al-Kutub, 1364 A.H.), s.v. *ʿibra.*

40. See ʿAbd al-Razzāq al-Qāshānī al-Samarqandī, *Istilāḥāt al-ṣūfiyya,* ed. Muḥammad Kamāl Ibrāhīm Jaʿfar (Cairo: al-Hay'a al-Miṣriyya al-ʿĀmma li'l-Kitāb, 1981), 130–31.

41. ʿAlī b. Wafā', *al-Bāʿith ʿalā'l-khalāṣ,* fol. 18v–19v.

42. *Wa man naẓara bi-qalb salīm ghayr dhī ʿiwaj ilā ṭarf min al-aṭrāf ẓahara lahu mā qulnāhu in shā'a allāh lakum taʿālāʿalā anna ḥaml al-kalām min al-muslim fi'l-muslim ʿalā aḥsan wujūhihi shān al-muttaqīn wa hadhā maʿrūf ḥattā fi-man ta'awwala kalām allāh wa rasūlihi maʿa ikhtilāf qulūbihim.* ʿAlī b. Wafā', *al-Bāʿith ʿalā'l-khalāṣ,* fol. 20r–21r; the passage quoted is found on fol. 21r.

43. Ibid., fol. 34r–v. On dreams and visions generally, see Toufic Fahd, *La Divination arabe: Études religieuses, sociologiques et folkloriques sur le mileu natif de l'islam* (Leiden: E. J. Brill, 1966), 247–367; idem, "The Dream in Medieval Islamic Society," in *The Dream and Human Societies,* ed. G. E. Von Grunebaum and Roger Caillois (Berkeley: University of California Press, 1966), 351–63; idem, "RU'YĀ," *EI,* 2d ed.; Yohanan Friedmann, *Prophecy Continuous: Aspects of Aḥmadī Religious Thought and Its Medieval Background* (Berkeley: University of California Press, 1989), 83–86; G. E. Von Grunebaum, "The Cultural Function of the Dream as Illustrated by Classical Islam," in Grunebaum and Caillois, *Dream and Human Societies,* 3–21; Jonathan G. Katz, "Visionary Experience, Autobiography, and

Sainthood in North African Islam," *Princeton Papers in Near Eastern Studies* 1 (1992): 85–118; idem, *Dreams, Sufism and Sainthood: The Visionary Career of Muḥammad al-Zawāwī* (Leiden: E. J. Brill, 1996), esp. 205–30; and Leah Kinberg, *Morality in the Guise of Dreams: A Critical Edition of Kitāb al-Manām with Introduction* (Leiden: E. J. Brill, 1994).

44. Katz, *Dreams, Sufism and Sainthood,* 213–14.

45. al-Bukhārī, *Ṣaḥīḥ,* "Kitāb al-Taʿbīr," no. 10; see also Aḥmad b. Ḥajar al-ʿAsqalānī, *Fatḥ al-bārī bi-sharḥ ṣaḥīḥ al-bukhārī,* ed. ʿAbd al-ʿAzīz b. ʿAbd Allāh b. Bāz, 15 vols. (Beirut: Dār al-Fikr, 1995), 14:410.

46. Jalāl al-Dīn al-Suyūṭī, *Tanwīr al-ḥalak fī imkān ru'yat al-nabī wa'l-malak,* in idem, *al-Ḥāwī li'l-fatāwī,* 2 vols. (Beirut: Dār al-Kutub al-ʿIlmiyya, 1983), 2:261. On traditions supporting this view, see Leah Kinberg, "Literal Dreams and Prophetic *Ḥadīṯs* in Classical Islam—A Comparison of Two Ways of Legitimation," *Der Islam* 70 (1993): 285n.

47. Henri Corbin, "The Visionary Dream in Islamic Spirituality," in Grunebaum and Caillois, *Dream and Human Societies,* 381–408; Kinberg, *Morality in the Guise of Dreams,* 35–36.

48. al-Bukhārī, *Ṣaḥīḥ,* "Kitāb al-Taʿbīr," *Bāb* 4; Ibn Ḥajar al-ʿAsqalānī, *Fatḥ al-bārī,* 14:399. For other versions, see A. J. Wensinck, *Concordances et indices de la tradition musulmane* (Leiden: E. J. Brill, 1943), 1:343, s.v. *juz',* and 2:205, s.v. *ru'yā.*

49. al-Suyūṭī, *Taḥdhīr al-khawāṣṣ,* 139–41.

50. al-Suyūṭī, *Tanwīr al-ḥalak,* 2:260–61.

51. Leah Kinberg, "The Legitimization of the *Madhāhib* through Dreams," *Arabica* 32 (1985): 47–79.

52. Ironically, one of the targets of al-Zawāwī's attempt to legitimize himself through dreams was ʿAlī b. Wafā's grandson, Yaḥyā, and other Wafā'ī shaykhs (Katz, *Dreams, Sufism, and Sainthood,* 122–30).

53. ʿUmar b. ʿAlī b. al-Mulaqqin, *Ṭabaqāt al-awliyā',* ed. Nūr al-Dīn Shurayba (Cairo: al-Khāngī, 1994), 439–40. There is some confusion over Ibn Abī Jamra's date of death.

54. Abū Muḥammad ʿAbd Allāh b. Saʿd b. Abī Jamra, *Kitāb al-marā'ī,* B.L. Add. Ms. 23,262, fol. 4r. Jonathan Katz discussed this work in "Visionary Experience, Autobiography, and Sainthood," 89–92.

55. ʿAbd al-Wahhāb al-Shaʿrānī, *al-Ṭabaqāt al-kubrā,* 2 vols. (Cairo: Muḥammad ʿAlī Ṣubayḥ, 1965), 1:176.

56. Mālik b. Anas, *al-Muwaṭṭa'* (Beirut: Dār al-Jīl, 1993), 829–31; al-Bukhārī,

Ṣaḥīḥ, "Kitāb al-Taʿbīr," no. 5; Ibn Ḥajar al-ʿAsqalānī, *Fatḥ al-bārī,* 14:401–2; Wensinck, *Concordances,* 6:338, s.v. *nubuwwa.*

57. Ibn Ḥajar al-ʿAsqalānī, *Fatḥ al-bārī,* 14:465–69; Kinberg, "Literal Dreams and Prophetic *Ḥadīṯs,*" 286–87; idem, *Morality in the Guise of Dreams,* 47–48.

58. ʿAlī b. Wafā', *al-Bāʿith ʿalāʾl-khalāṣ,* fol. 31r–v; see also Muslim, *Ṣaḥīḥ,* "Kitāb al-ru'yā," no. 3; Wensinck, *Concordances,* 2:206, s.v. *ru'yā'.*

59. ʿAlī b. Wafā', *al-Bāʿith ʿalā' l-khalāṣ,* fol. 30v–31r.

60. Abū'l-Laṭā'if b. Fāris, *al-Minaḥ al-ilāhiyya fī manāqib al-sādāt al-wafā'iyya,* B.N. ms. arabe 1200, fol. 21v–22r; see also al-Suyūṭī, *Tanwīr al-ḥalak,* in idem, *al-Ḥāwī li'l-fatāwī,* 2:261.

61. Aḥmad b. Muḥammad b. Khallikān, *Wafayāt al-aʿyān wa-anbā' abnā' al-zamān,* ed. Iḥsan ʿAbbās, 8 vols. (Beirut: Dār Ṣādir, 1978), 3:156–57; MacGuckin de Slane, *Ibn Khallikan's Biographical Dictionary,* 4 vols. (Paris: Oriental Translation Fund of Great Britain and Ireland, 1842–71), 2:110–11; MacGuckin de Slane, "Notice sur Ibn-Nobata, le plus grand prédicateur des Arabes," *Journal Asiatique,* 3d ser., 9 (1840): 66–77.

62. See Kinberg, "Legitimization of the *Madhāhib.*"

63. ʿAlī b. Wafā', *al-Bāʿith ʿalāʾl-khalāṣ,* fol. 31v–32r. Al-ʿIrāqī's concern that those experiencing dreams and visions might perceive something that contravened the *sharīʿa* was widely held. See, for example, Ibn al-Ḥājj, *Madkhal al-sharʿ al-sharīf,* 4:286; cf. Katz, "Visionaries, Autobiography, and Sainthood," 91.

64. Ibid., fol. 33r–34v.

65. Ibid., fol. 29v–30r.

66. George Makdisi, "Ibn Taimīya: A Ṣūfi of the Qādiriya Order," *American Journal of Arabic Studies* 1 (1974): 128; Th. Emil Homerin, "Sufis and Their Detractors in Mamluk Egypt: A Survey of Protagonists and Institutional Settings," *Islamic Mysticism Contested: Thirteen Centuries of Controversies and Polemics,* ed. Frederick De Jong and Bernd Radtke (Leiden: Brill, 1999), 234. Of course, divine inspiration of favored individuals (*ilḥām*) was to be distinguished from *waḥy,* the revelation that God conveyed to prophets. The latter carried with it law and was addressed to humankind in general; the former was usually understood to be specifically addressed to the individual inspired. See *EI,* 2d ed., art. "ILḤĀM" (by D. B. MacDonald). Nonetheless, ʿAlī b. Wafā'—and Ibn Taymiyya as well?—seems to perceive in *ilḥām* a means of conveying messages which, though channeled through the individual recipient, might speak to Muslims more generally.

67. ʿAlī b. Wafā', *al-Bāʿith ʿalāʾl-khalāṣ,* fol. 30r–v.

5 / CONCLUSION: STORYTELLING, PREACHING, AND THE PROBLEM OF RELIGIOUS AUTHORITY IN MEDIEVAL ISLAM

1. See, for example, Patricia Crone and Martin Hinds, *God's Caliph: Religious Authority in the First Centuries of Islam* (Cambridge: Cambridge University Press, 1986).

2. Richard Bulliet, *Conversion to Islam in the Medieval Period* (Cambridge, Mass.: Harvard University Press, 1979), 40. Much of my thinking on this subject has been shaped by Bulliet's brilliant recent essay, *Islam: The View from the Edge* (New York: Columbia University Press, 1994).

3. This is one of the central themes of Bulliet, *Islam,* esp. 180–83.

4. Joseph Schacht, *An Introduction to Islamic Law* (Oxford: Clarendon Press, 1964), 69f, esp. 70.

5. See especially Wael Hallaq, "Was the Gate of *Ijtihād* Closed?" *International Journal of Middle East Studies* 16 (1984): 3–41.

6. See, for example, Elizabeth Sartain's account of Jalāl al-Dīn al-Suyūṭī's claims, and the reaction to them, at the end of the Mamluk period: *Jalāl al-Dīn al-Suyūṭī,* 2 vols., vol. 1: *Biography and Background* (Cambridge: Cambridge University Press, 1975), 61–71.

7. See, for example, Sherman A. Jackson, *Islamic Law and the State: The Constitutional Jurisprudence of Shihāb al-Dīn al-Qarāfī* (Leiden: E. J. Brill, 1996); and Mohammad Fadel, "The Social Logic of *Taqlīd* and the Rise of the *Mukhtaṣar,*" *Islamic Law and Society* 3 (1996): 193–233.

8. Jackson, *Islamic Law and the State,* 77.

9. Paul Nwyia, *Ibn ʿAṭā' Allāh (m. 709/1309) et la naissance de la confrérie šāḏilite* (Beirut: Dar el-Machreq, 1972), 23–24.

10. Jonathan Berkey, *The Transmission of Knowledge in Medieval Cairo: A Social History of Islamic Education* (Princeton: Princeton University Press, 1992), 56–60.

11. See, for example, George Makdisi, "Ibn Taimīya: A Ṣūfī of the Qādiriya Order," *American Journal of Arabic Studies* 1 (1974): 118–29; and idem, "The Hanbali School and Sufism," *Boletin de la Asociacion Espanola de Orientalistas* 15 (1979): 115–26.

12. Michael Winter, *Society and Religion in Early Ottoman Egypt: Studies in the Writings of ʿAbd al-Wahhāb al-Shaʿrānī* (New Brunswick, N.J.: Transaction Books, 1982), 192–95, 230–36. It is largely because of conversations with Professor Winter that I have tempered somewhat my earlier enthusiasm for the notion of a rapprochement between Sufism and jurisprudential Islam.

13. Muhsin Mahdi, "The Book and the Master as Poles of Cultural Change in Islam," in *Islam and Cultural Change in the Middle Ages,* ed. Speros Vryonis Jr. (Wiesbaden: Otto Harrassowitz, 1975), 3–15, esp. 6–9.

14. See Marshall G. S. Hodgson, *The Venture of Islam: Conscience and History in a World Civilization,* vol. 2: *The Expansion of Islam in the Middle Periods* (Chicago: University of Chicago Press, 1974), 192–200.

15. See, for example, George Saliba, *A History of Arabic Astronomy: Planetary Theories during the Golden Age of Islam* (New York: New York University Press, 1994). Saliba's studies focus on the eleventh to fifteenth centuries, and the use of the phrase *Golden Age of Islam* in his subtitle was chosen deliberately to make the point that this period, rather than the earlier "classical" era, saw significant advances in this particular area of the natural sciences.

16. Gilsenan, *Recognizing Islam,* 27–30; Eric Hobsbawm, "Inventing Traditions," in *The Invention of Tradition,* ed. Eric Hobsbawm and Terence Ranger (Cambridge: Cambridge University Press, 1983), 2–3.

17. Fadel, "Social Logic of *Taqlīd,*" esp. 225–26.

18. I have discussed this polemic, and certain methodological issues bearing on medieval Islamic history which stem from it, in more detail in "Tradition, Innovation, and the Social Construction of Knowledge in the Medieval Islamic Near East," *Past and Present* 146 (1995): 38–65.

19. See, for example, Roy Mottahedeh's groundbreaking work *Loyalty and Leadership in an Early Islamic Society* (Princeton: Princeton University Press, 1980).

Works Cited

PRIMARY SOURCES

ʿAlī b. Muḥammad b. Wafā' [listed in the Catalogue as "Anonymous"]. *al-Bāiʿth ʿalā'l-khalāṣ min sū' al-ẓann bi'l-khawāṣ.* B.L. Or. Ms. 4275.

ʿAlī Pasha Mubārak. *al-Khiṭaṭ al-tawfīqiyya al-jadīda li-miṣr wa'l-qāhira.* 20 vols. Būlāq: al-Maṭbaʿa al-Kubrā al-Amīriyya, 1305 A.H.

Anonymous. B.L. Or. Ms. 7528.

al-Baghdādī, ʿAbd al-Qāhir b. Ṭāhir. *al-Farq bayna 'l-firaq,* ed. Ṭaha ʿAbd al-Ra'ūf Saʿd. Cairo: al-Ḥalabī, n.d.

al-Bayḍāwī, ʿAbd Allāh b. ʿUmar. *Anwār al-tanzīl wa-asrār al-ta'wīl.* 2 vols. Beirut: Dār al-Kutub al-ʿIlmiyya, 1988.

al-Ghazālī, Abū Ḥāmid. *Iḥyā' ʿulūm al-dīn.* 5 vols. Cairo: al-Ḥalabī, 1968. (Portions trans. T. J. Winter. *The Remembrance of Death and the Afterlife.* Cambridge: Islamic Texts Society, 1989.)

al-Ḥarīrī, Qāsim b. ʿAlī. *Maqāmāt.* Beirut: Dār Ṣādir, 1980. (Trans. T. Chenery, *The Assemblies of al-Ḥarīrī,* vol. 1. London: Williams and Northgate, 1867. Trans. F. Steinglass, *The Assemblies of al-Ḥarīrī,* vol. 2. London: S. Low, Marston, 1898.)

al-Ḥurayfīsh, ʿAbd Allāh b. Saʿd Allāh. *al-Rawḍ al-fā'iq fi'l-mawāʿiẓ wa'l-raqā'iq.* Cairo: Muṣṭafā al-Bābī al-Ḥalabī, 1949.

Ibn Abī Jamra, Abū Muḥammad ʿAbd Allāh b. Saʿd. *Kitāb al-marā'ī,* B.L. Add. Ms. 23,262.

Ibn al-Athīr, ʿAlī b. Muḥammad. *al-Kāmil fi'l-tārīkh,* ed. Yūsuf al-Daqqāq. 10 vols. Beirut: Dār al-Kutub al-ʿIlmiyya, 1995.

Ibn Fāris, Abū'l-Laṭā'if. *al-Minaḥ al-ilāhiyya fī manāqib al-sādāt al-wafā'iyya,* B.N. Ms. arabe 1200.

Ibn al-Furāt, Muḥammad b. ʿAbd al-Raḥīm. *Tārīkh,* ed. Qusṭanṭīn Zurayq and Najlā ʿIzz al-Dīn, vols. 7–9. Beirut: American University in Beirut Press, 1936–42.

Ibn Ḥajar al-ʿAsqalānī, Aḥmad. *al-Durar al-kāmina fī aʿyān al-miʾa al-thāmina,* ed. Muḥammad Sayyid Jād al-Ḥaqq. 5 vols. Cairo: Dār al-Kutub al-Ḥadītha, 1966.

———. *Fatḥ al-bārī bi-sharḥ ṣaḥīḥ al-bukhārī,* ed. ʿAbd al-ʿAzīz b. Bāz. 16 vols. Beirut: Dār al-Fikr, 1995.

———. *Inbāʾ al-ghumr bi-abnāʾ al-ʿumr.* 9 vols. Haydarabad: Dāʾirat al-Maʿārif al-ʿUthmāniyya, 1975.

Ibn al-Ḥājj al-ʿAbdarī. *Madkhal al-sharʿ al-sharīf.* 4 vols. Cairo: al-Maṭbaʿa al-Miṣriyya, 1929.

Ibn al-ʿImād, ʿAbd al-Ḥayy b. Aḥmad. *Shadharāt al-dhahab fī akhbār man dhahab.* 8 vols. Cairo: Maktabat al-Qudsī, 1931–32.

Ibn Isḥaq. *Sīrat rasūl allāh,* trans. Alfred Guillaume. *The Life of Muhammad.* Oxford: Oxford University Press, 1955.

Ibn al-Jawzī, ʿAbd al-Raḥmān b. ʿAlī. *Kitāb al-luṭf fī'l-waʿẓ.* Beirut: Dār al-Kutub al-ʿIlmiyya, 1984.

———. *Kitāb al-mawḍūʿāt,* 2d ed., ed. ʿAbd al-Raḥmān Muḥammad ʿUthmān. 3 vols. Cairo: Dār al-Fikr, 1983.

———. *Kitāb al-quṣṣāṣ wa'l-mudhakkirīn,* ed. and trans. Merlin Swartz. Beirut: Dar al-Machreq, 1986.

———. *al-Muntaẓam fī tārīkh al-mulūk wa'l-umam.* 10 vols. Haydarabad: Dāʾirat al-Maʿārif al-ʿUthmāniyya, 1359 A.H.

———. *Ṣayd al-khāṭir,* ed. Adam Abū Sunayna. Amman: Maktabat Dār al-Fikr, 1987.

———. *Talbīs iblīs.* Beirut: Dār al-Kutub al-ʿIlmiyya, n.d.

———. *al-Yāqūta fī'l-waʿẓ.* Cairo: ʿĪsā al-Bābī al-Ḥalabī, 1351 A.H.

Ibn Jubayr, Muḥammad b. Aḥmad. *Riḥla.* Beirut: Dār Ṣādir, 1980.

Ibn Kathīr, Ismāʿīl b. ʿUmar. *al-Bidāya wa'l-nihāya.* 14 vols. Cairo: Maṭbaʿat al-Saʿāda, 1932–39.

———. *Qiṣaṣ al-anbiyāʾ,* ed. ʿAbd al-Muʿṭī ʿAbd al-Maqṣūd Muḥammad. Alexandria: Maktabat Ḥamīdū, 1990.

———. *Tafsīr al-qurʾān al-ʿaẓīm.* 4 vols. Beirut: Dār al-Maʿrifa, 1995.

Ibn Khaldūn, ʿAbd al-Raḥmān b. Muḥammad. *The Muqaddimah,* 2d ed., trans. Franz Rosenthal. 3 vols. Princeton: Princeton University Press, 1980.

Ibn Khallikān, Aḥmad b. Muḥammad. *Wafayāt al-aʿyān wa anbāʾ abnāʾ al-zamān,* ed. Iḥsān ʿAbbās. 8 vols. Beirut: Dār Ṣādir, 1978. (Trans. MacGuckin de Slane.

Ibn Khallikan's Biographical Dictionary. 4 vols. Paris: Oriental Translation Fund of Great Britain and Ireland, 1842.)

Ibn al-Mulaqqin, ʿUmar b. ʿAlī. *Ṭabaqāt al-awliyā',* ed. Nūr al-Dīn Shurayba. Cairo: al-Khāngī, 1994.

Ibn Nubāta al-Fāriqī, ʿAbd al-Raḥīm b. Muḥammad. *Dīwān khuṭab.* Beirut: Maṭbaʿat Jarīdat Bayrūt, 1311 A.H.

Ibn Qāḍī Shuhba, Abū Bakr b. Aḥmad. *Ṭabaqāt al-shāfiʿiyya.* 4 vols. Haydarabad: Dā'irat al-Maʿārif al-ʿUthmāniyya, 1979.

Ibn Rajab, Abū'l-Faraj ʿAbd al-Raḥmān b. Aḥmad. *Kitāb al-dhayl ʿalā ṭabaqāt al-ḥanābila,* ed. Muḥammad Ḥāmid al-Fiqī. 2 vols. Cairo: Maktabat al-Sunna al-Muḥammadiyya, 1952–53.

Ibn al-Ṣalāḥ al-Shahrazūrī, *ʿUlūm al-ḥadīth,* ed. Nūr al-Dīn ʿAtar. Beirut: Dār al-Fikr, 1984.

Ibn al-Ṣayrafī al-Jawharī, ʿAlī b. Dā'ūd. *Nuzhat al-nufūs wa'l-abdān fī tawārīkh al-zamān,* ed. Ḥasan Ḥabashī. Cairo: Wizārat al-Thaqāfa, 1970–.

Ibn Taghrī Birdī, Abū'l-Maḥāsin Yūsuf. *al-Manhal al-ṣāfī wa'l-mustawfī baʿd al-wāfī,* ed. Muḥammad M. Amīn. 7 vols. to date. Cairo: al-Hay'a al-Miṣriyya al-ʿĀmma li'l-Kitāb, 1984–.

———. *al-Nujūm al-zāhira fī mulūk miṣr wa'l-qāhira.* 16 vols. Cairo: al-Mu'assasa al-Miṣriyya al-ʿĀmma li'l-Ta'līf wa'l-Ṭibāʿa wa'l-Nashr, 1963–71.

Ibn Taymiyya, Aḥmad. *Aḥādīth al-quṣṣāṣ,* ed. Muḥammad al-Ṣabbāgh. Beirut: al-Maktab al-Islāmī, 1972.

Ibn al-Ukhuwwa, Ḍiyā' al-Dīn Muḥammad. *Maʿālim al-qurba fī aḥkām al-ḥisba,* ed. Reuben Levy. E. J. W. Gibb Memorial Series, n.s., 12. Cambridge: Cambridge University Press, 1938.

al-Idrīsī, ʿAlī b. Maymūn. *Bayān ghurbat al-islām bi-wāsiṭat ṣinfay al-mutafaqqiha wa'l-mutafaqqira min ahl miṣr wa'l-shām wa mā yalīhima min bilād al-aʿjām.* Princeton Garret Ms. 828H.

al-Jāḥiẓ, Abū 'Uthmān ʿAmr b. Baḥr. *al-Bayān wa'l-tabyīn,* ed. ʿAbd al-Salām Muḥammad Hārūn. 4 vols. Cairo: al-Khāngī, 1975.

al-Jawbarī, ʿAbd al-Raḥīm b. ʿUmar. *al-Mukhtār min kashf al-asrār.* Damascus, 1302 A.H. Trans. René Khawam. *Le voile arraché.* Paris: Phebus, 1979.

al-Khaṭīb al-Baghdādī, Abū Bakr Aḥmad b. ʿAlī. *Tārīkh baghdād.* 14 vols. Beirut: Dār al-Kitāb al-ʿArabī, 1966.

al-Makkī, Abū Ṭālib, *Qūt al-qulūb fī muʿāmalat al-maḥbūb wa-waṣf ṭarīq al-murīd ilā maqām al-tawḥīd,* ed. Bāsil ʿUyūn al-Sūd, 2 vols. Beirut: Dār al-Kutub al-ʿIlmiyya, 1997.

Mālik b. Anas. *al-Muwaṭṭa'*. Beirut. Dār al-Jīl, 1993.

al-Maqrīzī, Aḥmad b. ʿAlī. *al-Sulūk li-maʿrifat duwal al-mulūk*, ed. Muḥammad Muṣṭafā Ziyāda and Saʿīd ʿAbd al-Fattāḥ ʿĀshūr. 4 vols. in 12. Cairo: Lajnat al-Ta'līf wa'l-Tarjama wa'l-Nashr, 1956–73.

al-Nawawī, Muḥyī 'l-Dīn Abū Zakariyyā. *Sharḥ ṣaḥīḥ muslim*. 18 vols. in 6. Beirut: Mu'assasat Manāhil al-ʿIrfān, n.d.

al-Qalqashandī, Aḥmad b. ʿAlī. *Ṣubḥ al-aʿshā fī ṣināʿat al-inshā'*. 14 vols. Cairo: al-Mu'assasa al-Miṣriyya al-ʿĀmma li'l-Ta'līf wa'l-Tarjama wa'l-Ṭibāʿa wa'l-Nashr, 1964.

al-Qāshānī al-Samarqandī, ʿAbd al-Razzāq. *Istilāḥāt al-ṣūfiyya*, ed. Muḥammad Kamāl Ibrāhīm Jaʿfar. Cairo: al-Hay'a al-Miṣriyya al-ʿĀmma li'l-Kitāb, 1981.

al-Ṣafadī, Khalīl b. Aybak, *al-Wāfī bi'l-wafiyyāt*, 2d ed. Wiesbaden: Frank Steiner Verlag, 1962–.

al-Sakhāwī, Muḥammad b. ʿAbd al-Raḥmān. *al-Ḍaw' al-lāmiʿ li-ahl al-qarn al-tāsiʿ*. 12 vols. Cairo: Maktabat al-Quds, 1934.

———. *al-Maqāṣid al-ḥasana fī bayān kathīr min al-aḥādīth al-mushtahara ʿalā'l-alsina*, ed. ʿAbd Allāh Muḥammad al-Ṣadīq. Cairo: al-Khāngī, 1991.

———. *al-Tibr al-masbūk li-dhayl al-sulūk*. Cairo: Maktabat al-Kulliyāt al-Azhariyya, n.d.

al-Shahrastānī, Muḥammad b. ʿAbd al-Karīm. *Kitāb al-milal wa'l-niḥal*, ed. ʿAbd al-ʿAzīz Muḥammad al-Wakīl. 3 vols. Cairo: al-Ḥalabī, n.d. Trans. A. K. Kazi and J. G. Flynn, *Muslim Sects and Divisions*. London: Kegan Paul, 1984.

al-Shaʿrānī, Tāj al-Dīn ʿAbd al-Wahhāb. *al-Ṭabaqāṭ al-kubrā*. 2 vols. Cairo: Muḥammad ʿAlī Ṣubayḥ, 1965.

———. *al-Ṭabaqāt al-ṣughrā*, ed. ʿAbd al-Qādir Aḥmad ʿAtā. Cairo: Maktabat al-Qāhira, 1970.

Sibṭ b. al-Jawzī, Abū'l-Muẓaffar Yūsuf. *Mir'āt al-zamān fī tārīkh al-aʿyān*, vol. 8 in 2. Haydarabad: Dā'irat al-Maʿārif al-ʿUthmāniyya, 1951–52.

al-Subkī, Tāj al-Dīn ʿAbd al-Wahhāb. *Muʿīd al-niʿam wa mubīd al-niqam*, ed. David W. Myhrman. London: Luzac, 1908.

———. *Ṭabaqāt al-shāfiʿiyya al-kubrā*, 2d ed., ed. ʿAbd al-Fattāḥ Muḥammad al-Hilw and Maḥmūd Muḥammad al-Ṭanāhī. 10 vols. Cairo: Hajar, 1992.

al-Suyūṭī, Jalāl al-Dīn. *al-Ḥāwī li'l-fatāwī*. 2 vols. Beirut: Dār al-Kutub al-ʿIlmiyya, 1983.

———. *Taḥdhīr al-khawāṣṣ min akādhīb al-quṣṣāṣ*, ed. Muḥammad al-Ṣabbāgh. Beirut: al-Maktab al-Islāmī, 1972.

al-Thaʿlabī, Aḥmad b. Muḥammad. *Qiṣaṣ al-anbiyā' al-musammā bi'l-ʿarā'is*. Cairo: Maktabat al-Jumhūriyya al-ʿArabiyya, n.d.

al-Turkumānī, Idrīs b. Baydakīn. *Kitāb al-lumaʿ fi'l-ḥawādith wa'l-bidaʿ*, ed. Ṣubḥī Labīb. Wiesbaden: Franz Steiner Verlag, 1986.

al-Ṭurṭūshī, Abū Bakr Muḥammad. *Kitāb al-ḥawādith wa'l-bidaʿ*, ed. A. M. Turki. Beirut: Dār al-Gharb al-Islāmī, 1990.

SECONDARY SOURCES

ʿAbd al-Bāqī, Muḥammad Fu'ād. *al-Muʿjam al-mufahras li-alfāẓ al-qur'ān al-karīm.* Cairo: Dār al-Kutub, 1364 A.H.

Adang, Camilla. *Muslim Writers on Judaism and the Hebrew Bible from Ibn Rabban to Ibn Hazm.* Leiden: E. J. Brill, 1996.

al-Bakrī, Muḥammad Tawfīq. *Kitāb bayt al-sādāt al-wafā'iyya.* Cairo: n.p., n.d.

Asad, Talal. *Genealogies of Religion: Discipline and Reasons of Power in Christianity and Islam.* Baltimore: Johns Hopkins University Press, 1993.

Athamina, Khalil. "Al-Qasas: Its Emergence, Religious Origin and Its Socio-political Impact on Early Muslim Society." *Studia Islamica* 76 (1992): 53–74.

Awn, Peter J. *Satan's Tragedy and Redemption: Iblīs in Sufi Psychology.* Leiden: E. J. Brill, 1983.

Ayoub, Mahmoud. *The Qur'an and Its Interpreters,* vol. 1. Albany: SUNY Press, 1984.

Berkey, Jonathan P. "Tradition, Innovation, and the Social Construction of Knowledge in the Medieval Islamic Near East." *Past and Present* 146 (1995): 38–65.

———. *The Transmission of Knowledge in Medieval Cairo: A Social History of Islamic Education.* Princeton: Princeton University Press, 1992.

Bosworth, C. E. "Jewish Elements in the Banū Sāsān." *Bibliotheca Orientalis* 33 (1976): 289–94.

———. *The Medieval Islamic Underground: The Banū Sāsān in Arabic Society and Literature,* 2 vols. Leiden: E. J. Brill, 1976.

Brinner, William. "The Significance of the *Ḥarāfīsh* and Their 'Sultan.'" *JESHO* 6 (1963): 190–215.

Bulliet, Richard W. *The Patricians of Nishapur: A Study in Medieval Islamic Social History.* Cambridge, Mass.: Harvard University Press, 1972.

———. *Islam: The View from the Edge.* New York: Columbia University Press, 1994.

Chamberlain, Michael. *Knowledge and Social Practice in Damascus, 1190–1350.* Cambridge: Cambridge University Press, 1994.

Corbin, Henri. "The Visionary Dream in Islamic Spirituality." In *The Dream and Human Societies,* ed. G. E. Von Grunebaum and Roger Caillois, 381–408. Berkeley: University of California Press, 1966.

Crone, Patricia. *Meccan Trade and the Rise of Islam.* Oxford: Basil Blackwell, 1987.

Crone, Patricia, and Martin Hinds. *God's Caliph: Religious Authority in the First Centuries of Islam.* Cambridge: Cambridge University Press, 1986.

Davis, Natalie Zemon. *Fiction in the Archives: Pardon Tales and Their Tellers in Sixteenth-Century France.* Stanford: Stanford University Press, 1987.

———. "From 'Popular Religion' to Religious Culture." In *Reformation Europe: A Guide to Research,* ed. Steven Ozment, 321–41. St. Louis: Center for Reformation Research, 1982.

De Jong, F. *Ṭuruq and Ṭuruq-Linked Institutions in Nineteenth-Century Egypt: A Historical Study in Organizational Dimensions of Islamic Mysticism.* Leiden: E. J. Brill, 1978.

De Slane, MacGuckin. "Notice sur Ibn-Nobata, le plus grand prédicateur des Arabes." *Journal Asiatique,* 3d ser., 9 (1940): 66–77.

Donner, Fred M. *Narratives of Islamic Origins: The Beginnings of Islamic Historical Writing.* Princeton: Darwin Press, 1998.

Duri, A. A. *The Rise of Historical Writing among the Arabs,* trans. Lawrence Conrad. Princeton: Princeton University Press, 1983.

Fadel, Mohammad. "The Social Logic of *Taqlīd* and the Rise of the *Mukhtaṣar.*" *Islamic Law and Society* 3 (1996): 193–233.

Fahd, Toufic. *La Divination arabe: Études religieuses, sociologiques et folkloriques sur le milieu natif de l'islam.* Leiden: E. J. Brill, 1966.

———. "The Dream in Medieval Islamic Society." In *The Dream and Human Societies,* ed. G. E. Von Grunebaum and Roger Caillois, 351–63. Berkeley: University of California Press, 1966.

Fierro, Maribel. "The Treatises against Innovations (*kutub al-bidʿa*)." *Der Islam* 69 (1992): 204–46.

Finkel, Joshua. "An Arabic Story of Abraham." *Hebrew Union College Annual* 12–13 (1938): 387–409.

Firestone, Reuven. *Journeys in Holy Lands: The Evolution of the Abraham-Ishmael Legends in Islamic Exegesis.* Albany: SUNY Press, 1990.

Friedlander, Israel. "A Muhammedan Book on Augury in Hebrew Characters." *Jewish Quarterly Review,* n.s., 19 (1917): 84–103.

Friedmann, Yohanan. *Prophecy Continuous: Aspects of Aḥmadī Religious Thought and Its Medieval Background.* Berkeley: University of California Press, 1989.

Gaffney, Patrick. *The Prophet's Pulpit: Islamic Preaching in Contemporary Egypt.* Berkeley: University of California Press, 1994.

Garcin, Jean-Claude. "Histoire, opposition politique et piétisme traditionaliste dans le *Ḥusn al-Muḥādarat* de Suyūṭī." *Annales Islamologiques* 7 (1967): 33–89.

Geertz, Clifford. *The Interpretation of Culture.* New York: Basic Books, 1973.

———. *Islam Observed: Religious Development in Morocco and Indonesia.* New Haven: Yale University Press, 1968.

Gerhardt, Mia I. *The Art of Storytelling: A Literary Study of the Thousand and One Nights.* Leiden: E. J. Brill, 1963.

Gilsenan, Michael. *Recognizing Islam: Religion and Society in the Modern Middle East.* London: I. B. Tauris, 1992.

Goldziher, Ignaz. *Muslim Studies,* trans. C. R. Barber and S. M. Stern. 2 vols. London: George Allen and Unwin, 1966.

Grabar, Oleg. *Formation of Islamic Art.* New Haven: Yale University Press, 1973.

Graham, William A. *Divine Word and Prophetic Word in Early Islam: A Reconsideration of the Sources, with Special Reference to the Divine Saying or Ḥadīth Qudsī.* The Hague: Mouton, 1977.

Hallaq, Wael. "Was the Gate of *Ijtihād* Closed?" *International Journal of Middle East Studies* 16 (1984): 3–41.

Heath, Peter. *The Thirsty Sword: Sīrat ʿAntar and the Arabic Popular Epic.* Salt Lake City: University of Utah Press, 1996.

Hobsbawm, Eric. "Inventing Traditions." In *The Invention of Tradition,* ed. Eric Hobsbawm and Terence Ranger, 1–14. Cambridge: Cambridge University Press, 1983.

Hodgson, Marshall G. S. *The Venture of Islam: Conscience and History in a World Civilization.* 3 vols. Chicago: University of Chicago Press, 1974.

———. *Rethinking World History: Essays on Europe, Islam, and World History,* ed. Edmund Burke III. Cambridge: Cambridge University Press, 1993.

Homerin, Th. Emil. *From Arab Poet to Muslim Saint: Ibn al-Fāriḍ, His Verse, and His Shrine.* Columbia: University of South Carolina Press, 1994.

———. "Preaching Poetry: The Forgotten Verse of Ibn al-Shahrazūrī." *Arabica* 38 (1991): 87–101.

———. "Sufis and Their Detractors in Mamluk Egypt. A Survey of Protagonists and Institutional Settings." In *Islamic Mysticism Contested: Thirteen Centuries of Controversies and Polemics,* ed. Frederick De Jong and Bernd Radtke, 225–47. Leiden: E. J. Brill, 1999.

Humphreys, R. Stephen. *From Saladin to the Mongols: The Ayyubids of Damascus, 1193–1260.* Albany: SUNY Press, 1977.

Juynboll, G. H. A. *Muslim Tradition: Studies in Chronology, Provenance, and Authorship of Early Ḥadīth.* Cambridge: Cambridge University Press, 1983.

Karamustafa, Ahmet. *God's Unruly Friends: Dervish Groups in the Islamic Later Middle Period, 1200–1500.* Salt Lake City: University of Utah Press 1994.

Katz, Jonathan G. *Dreams, Sufism and Sainthood: The Visionary Career of Muḥammad al-Zawāwī.* Leiden: E. J. Brill, 1996.

———. "Visionary Experience, Autobiography, and Sainthood in North African Islam." *Princeton Papers in Near Eastern Studies* 1 (1992): 85–118.

Khalidi, Tarif. *Islamic Historiography: The Histories of Masʿūdī.* Albany: SUNY Press, 1975.

Kinberg, Leah. "The Legitimization of the *Madhāhib* through Dreams." *Arabica* 32 (1985): 47–79.

———. "Literal Dreams and Prophetic *Ḥadīṯs* in Classical Islam—A Comparison of Two Ways of Legitimation." *Der Islam* 70 (1993): 279–300.

———. *Morality in the Guise of Dreams: A Critical Edition of Kitāb al-Manām with Introduction.* Leiden: E. J. Brill, 1994.

———. "What Is Meant by *Zuhd*?" *Studia Islamica* 61 (1985): 27–44.

Kister, M. J. "*Ḥaddithū ʿan banī isrāʾīla wa-lā ḥaraja:* A Study of an Early Tradition." *Israel Oriental Studies* 2 (1972): 215–39.

Knysh, Alexander. "'Orthodoxy' and 'Heresy' in Medieval Islam: An Essay in Reassessment." *Muslim World* 83 (1993): 48–67.

Krauss, Samuel. "A Moses Legend." *Jewish Quarterly Review,* n.s., 5 (1911–12): 339–64.

Lane, Edward William. *An Account of the Manners and Customs of the Modern Egyptians,* 5th ed. 1860. Reprint. New York: Dover, 1973.

Lassner, Jacob. *Demonizing the Queen of Sheba: Boundaries of Gender and Culture in Postbiblical Judaism and Medieval Islam.* Chicago: University of Chicago Press, 1993.

Lazarus-Yafeh, Hava. *Intertwined Worlds: Medieval Islam and Bible Criticism.* Princeton: Princeton University Press, 1992.

Leroy Ladurie, Emmanuel. *Montaillou: Promised Land of Error.* New York: George Braziller, 1978.

Lewis, Bernard. "The Question of Orientalism." *New York Review of Books,* 24 June 1982, 49–56.

———. "The Significance of Heresy in Islam." *Studia Islamica* 1 (1953): 43–63.

Lutfi, Huda. "Manners and Customs of Fourteenth-Century Cairene Women: Female Anarchy versus Male Sharʿi Order in Muslim Prescriptive Treatises." In *Women in Middle Eastern History: Shifting Boundaries in Sex and Gender,* ed. Nikki Keddie and Beth Baron, 99–121. New Haven: Yale University Press, 1991.

Mahdi, Muhsin. *Ibn Khaldūn's Philosophy of History.* Chicago: University of Chicago Press, 1964.

Makdisi, George. "The Hanbali School and Sufism." *Boletin de la Asociacion Espanola de Orientalistas* 15 (1979): 115–26.

———. "Ibn Taimīya: A Ṣūfi of the Qādiriya Order." *American Journal of Arabic Studies* 1 (1974): 118–29.

———. *Ibn ʿAqīl et la résurgence de l'Islam traditionaliste au XIe siècle (Ve siècle de l'Hégire).* Damascus: Institut Français de Damas, 1963.

———. "Muslim Institutions of Learning in Eleventh-Century Baghdad." *BSOAS* 24 (1961): 1–56.

———. *The Rise of Colleges: Institutions of Learning in Islam and the West.* Edinburgh: Edinburgh University Press, 1981.

Marlow, Louise. *Hierarchy and Egalitarianism in Islamic Thought.* Cambridge: Cambridge University Press, 1997.

Massignon, Louis. *Essai sur les origines du lexique technique de la mystique musulmane.* Paris: J. Vrin, 1954.

———. *The Passion of al-Hallāj: Mystic and Martyr of Islam,* trans. Herbert Mason. 4 vols. Princeton: Princeton University Press, 1982.

McAuliffe, Jane Dammen. "Assessing the *Isrā'īliyyāt:* An Exegetical Conundrum." In *Story-telling in the Framework of Non-fictional Arabic Literature,* ed. Stefan Leder, 245–69. Wiesbaden: Harrassowitz Verlag, 1998.

Memon, Muhammad Umar. *Ibn Taimiya's Struggle against Popular Religion.* The Hague: Mouton, 1976.

Mez, Adam. *The Renaissance of Islam,* trans. Salahuddin Khuda Bukhsh and D. S. Margoliouth. New York: AMS Press, 1975.

Nagel, Tilman. *Die Qiṣaṣ al-Anbiyā'. Ein Beitrag zur arabischen Literaturgeschichte.* Bonn: Rheinische Friedrich-Wilhems-Universität, 1967.

Newby, Gordon. "Tafsir Isra'iliyat: The Development of Qur'an Commentary in Early Islam in Its Relationship to Judaeo-Christian Traditions of Scriptural Commentary." In *Studies in Qur'an and Tafsir,* ed. Alford T. Welch, *Journal of the American Academy of Religion* 47, Thematic issue 4S (1980): 685–97.

Nöldeke, Theodor. *Sketches from Eastern History,* trans. John Sutherland Black. 1892. Reprint. Beirut: Khayats, 1963.

Pedersen, Johannes. "The Criticism of the Islamic Preacher." *Die Welt des Islams,* n.s., 2 (1953): 215–31.

———. "The Islamic Preacher: Wāʿiẓ, Mudhakkir, Qāṣṣ." *Ignace Goldziher Memorial Volume.* Budapest, 1948, I, 226–51.

Pellat, Charles. *Le Milieu baṣrien et la formation de Ǧāḥiẓ.* Paris: Librairie d'Amérique et d'Orient, 1953.

Petry, Carl. *The Civilian Elite of Cairo in the Later Middle Ages.* Princeton: Princeton University Press, 1981.

Pinault, David. *Story-telling Techniques in the Arabian Nights.* Leiden: E. J. Brill, 1992.

Rahman, Fazlur. *Major Themes of the Quran.* Minneapolis: Bibliotheca Islamica, 1980.

Rieu, Charles. *Supplement to the Catalogue of the Arabic Manuscripts in the British Museum.* London: Longmans, 1894.

Rispler, Vardit. "Toward a New Understanding of the Term *Bidʿa.*" *Der Islam* 68 (1991): 320–28.

Rosenthal, Franz. *A History of Muslim Historiography.* Leiden: E. J. Brill, 1968.

———. *Knowledge Triumphant: The Concept of Knowledge in Medieval Islam.* Leiden: E. J. Brill, 1970.

Said, Edward. *Orientalism.* New York: Vintage, 1978.

Sanders, Paula. *Ritual, Politics, and the City in Fatimid Cairo.* Albany: SUNY Press, 1994.

Sartain, Elizabeth. *Jalāl al-Dīn al-Suyūṭī,* 2 vols. Vol. 1: *Biography and Background.* Cambridge, UK: Cambridge University Press, 1975.

Schwarzbaum, Haim. *Biblical and Extra-Biblical Legends in Islamic Folk Literature.* Walldorf-Hessen: Verlag für Orientkunde Dr. H. Verndran, 1982.

Shoshan, Boaz. *Popular Culture in Medieval Cairo.* Cambridge: Cambridge University Press, 1993.

Sivan, Emmanuel. *L'Islam et la croisade: Idéologie et propagande dans les réactions musulmane aux croisades.* Paris: Librairie d'Amérique et d'Orient, 1968.

Stone, Lawrence. "The Revival of Narrative: Reflections on a New Old History." *Past and Present* 85 (1979): 3–24.

Swartz, Merlin L. *Ibn al-Jawzī's Kitāb al-Quṣṣāṣ wa'l-Mudhakkirīn.* Beirut: Dar el-Machreq, 1971.

Taylor, Christopher S. *In the Vicinity of the Righteous: Ziyāra and the Veneration of Muslim Saints in Late Medieval Egypt.* Leiden: E. J. Brill, 1998.

Thackston, Wheeler M. *The Tales of the Prophets of al-Kisa'i.* Boston: Twayne Publishers, 1978.

Trimingham, J. Spencer. *The Sufi Orders in Islam.* Oxford: Oxford University Press, 1971.

al-Ṭuʿmī, Muḥyī 'l-Dīn. *Ṭabaqāt al-shādhiliyya al-kubrā.* Beirut: Dār al-Jīl, 1996.

Vadet, Jean Claude. "Les idées d'un prédicateur de mosquée au XIVe siècle dans le Caire des Mamlouks." *Annales Islamologiques* 8 (1969): 63–69.

Von Grunebaum, G. E. "The Cultural Function of the Dream as Illustrated by Classical Islam." In *The Dream and Human Societies,* ed. G. E. Von Grunebaum and Roger Caillois, 3–21. Berkeley: University of California Press, 1966.

———. *Muhammadan Festivals.* 1951. Reprint. New York: Olive Branch Press, 1988.

Wasserstrom, Steven M. *Between Muslim and Jew: The Problem of Symbiosis under Early Islam.* Princeton: Princeton University Press, 1995.

Wensinck, A. J. *Concordances et indices de la tradition musulmane.* Leiden: E. J. Brill, 1943.

Winter, Michael. *Society and Religion in Early Ottoman Egypt: Studies in the Writings of ʿAbd al-Wahhāb al-Shaʿrānī.* New Brunswick, N.J.: Transaction Books, 1982.

Index